The
Bumper
Book
of Nature

The
Bumper
Book
of Nature

A User's Guide to the Outdoors

Stephen Moss

Color Illustrations by Patricia J. Wynne

HARMONY BOOKS
NEW YORK

Published in the United States by Harmony Books, an imprint of the
Crown Publishing Group, a division of Random House, Inc., New York.
www.crownpublishing.com

Harmony Books is a registered trademark and the Harmony Books colophon
is a trademark of Random House, Inc.

Originally published, in slightly different form, in Great Britain by Square Peg,
an imprint of the Random House Group, Limited, London, in 2009.

Library of Congress Cataloging-in-Publication Data

Moss, Stephen, 1960–
The bumper book of nature / Stephen Moss.—1st ed.
p.   cm.
1. Nature—Experiments—Juvenile literature.   2. Nature study—Activity
programs—Juvenile literature.   I. Title.
QH55.M67 2010
508.078—dc22   2009040111

ISBN 978-0-307-58999-6

Printed in China

Design by Friederik Huber

10 9 8 7 6 5 4 3 2 1

First U.S. Edition

For David and Martine Osario,
for allowing us to be free-range children
instead of cotton-wool kids

Contents

A note to parents x
A note to children xii

All Year Round

Build a den 2   Make a nature table 4
How to identify . . . trees 7   Climb a
tree 10   Hang upside down from the branch
of a tree 11   Make a rope swing from a
tree 12   Tell the age of a tree 15   Make a
bark rubbing 16   Listen to the heartbeat of a
tree 17   **How to identify . . . common
birds** 19   Look for owl pellets 22   Look for
mammal tracks and signs 24   Make a plaster
cast of an animal track 25   Grow mustard
and cress 27   Stand out in the rain 28
Sit or stand still for an hour, just watching and
listening 29   Go for a "blind walk" 30
Play Poohsticks 31   Roll down a hill 31
Feed the birds in your backyard 32   Keep a
nature notebook and diary 35   Go for a
walk in a graveyard 37   Three ways to find
which direction you are facing without using
a compass . . . 40   Go out into your
backyard at night 42   Time thunder
and lightning to work out how far away a storm
is 43   Count the colors of a rainbow 43
Skip stones across a lake or pond 44
Play hide-and-seek 45   Visit your local
wildlife sanctuary 46   Become a conservation
volunteer 47   Use nature to forecast
the weather 49

Summer

Collect caterpillars and watch them change into butterflies 100   Catch butterflies with a net 104   How to identify . . . butterflies 107   Go moth trapping 110   Watch damselflies and dragonflies 113   Give bumblebees a helping hand 116   Take a really close look at an ant colony 117   How to identify . . . bugs 119   Make a home for minibeasts 122   Lie down in long grass and stare at the sky 124   Become a bat detective 125   Collect birds' feathers 126   Make an old-fashioned quill pen 127   Spend the night in a tent in your backyard 128   Make a compost heap 128   Go on a city safari 131   How to identify . . . amphibians 135   Look for snakes and lizards 138   Pick (and eat) blackberries 141   Some easy blackberry recipes 142   How to identify . . . roadside flowers and plants 145   Naughty stuff 148   Things to do with wildflowers 150   How to identify . . . creatures in a rock pool 159   Beside the sea 162   Go sea fishing 171   Look for marine life: seabirds, seals, whales, and dolphins 172   Summer weather lore 176

Spring

Look for catkins 54   Listen for woodpeckers drumming 55   How to identify . . . birds of prey 57   Find the first spring flowers 60   Some recipes using spring flowers and plants 61   Go see displays of cherry blossoms 64   Look for squirrel dreys 66   Listen to the dawn chorus 67   Provide a home for purple martins 68   Identify different birdsong 70   Take a close look in a pond 72   How to identify . . . pond life 75   Collect frogs' eggs—and watch them change into frogs 78   How to identify . . . reptiles 81   Go on an Easter egg hunt 84   Dye your Easter eggs yellow using flowers 85   Have a snail race 86   Identify trees by their leaves 88   Dig for earthworms 89   Look for mad March hares 91   Find a bird's nest 93   Spring weather lore 96

Winter

Feed the ducks 222   How to identify . . .
ducks and waterbirds 223   Go pishing
to attract small birds 226   Search
for hibernating butterflies 227   Go
beachcombing along the tide line 228   Watch
the sun rise and set on the same day 231   Go
swimming in the sea in winter 232   How to
identify . . . marine mammals 233   Look
for winter wildlife 236   Take part in
the Christmas Bird Count 237   Make
maple syrup candy 238   Six things
to do when it snows . . . 240   Make a
snowman 240   Catch a snowflake on
your tongue 241   Look at a snowflake
through a magnifying glass 241   Make
snow angels 242   Slide down a slope on a
tray or garbage bag 244   Have a snowball
fight 244   How to identify . . . large
mammals 245   Winter weather lore 248

Useful contacts 252
Further reading 254
Acknowledgments 257

Fall

Collect and roast sweet chestnuts 180
Make jack-o'-lanterns for Halloween 181
Roast pumpkin seeds for a tasty snack 183
Apple bobbing 184   Watch birds feeding
on fruit and berries 185   How to
identify . . . coastal birds 187   Collect
pinecones and make them into Christmas
decorations 190   Go on a "fungal
foray" 190   Collect seeds and plant
them 192   Make leaf rubbings 195
Listen for owls calling 197   Look for spiders
in your house 198   Look for spiderwebs
on a fall morning 199   Make a woodpile
in your backyard 201   How to identify
. . . small mammals 203   Trap small
mammals 206   Observe deer during the
rutting season 206   Make a birdhouse 208
Dig a pond in your backyard 211   Plant a
native hedgerow in your backyard 213   How
to identify . . . medium-size mammals 215
Be blown by the wind 218   Fall weather
lore 218

A note to parents

(and grandparents, godparents, aunts and uncles, big brothers and sisters, friends of the family, teachers, and anyone else who wants to get our children back in touch with nature . . .)

When you think back to your own childhood, what do you remember? Did you climb trees, build dens, and go for hikes in the woods? Of course you did—that's how we entertained ourselves in the days before computer games, cell phones, and a TV in every child's bedroom.

We didn't have the gadgets, the opportunities, or the sheer variety of ways that today's children have to spend their spare time. So to stave off boredom, we begged our parents to let us go and play outside. Ball games in the street were just the start. Soon we were scrambling over the fence and into the woods, exploring nature for ourselves. Later on, during summer vacation, we were sent out with Mom's words ringing in our ears: "Take care—and be back home for supper!"

OK, so I'm making our childhoods sound like something out of *Hiawatha* or *Anne of Green Gables.* It wasn't always like that, of course. Sometimes we hurt ourselves—falling out of trees or grazing our knees. Sometimes we came home soaked through after being caught in the rain, and got a good telling off from Mom and Dad.

But all this time we were learning about nature: seeing tadpoles turn into frogs, picking flowers, or simply watching the birds we came across in our wanderings. And by climbing trees and building dens we also learned about taking risks, about working together as a team, and ultimately about our own limits.

So tell me, honestly: are today's children happier and more fulfilled than we were? Of course they aren't. In the past couple of decades, we have raised generations of children who are scared to walk in the park on their own, who scream when they encounter a spider or a moth, and who know more about the characters in TV shows than they do about our native animals and plants.

The consequences of this—what Californian writer Richard Louv has called Nature Deficit Disorder—are very worrying. If we're not careful, when these children grow up, they will have no interest in, or passion for, the natural world—and if you don't care about something, what incentive is there to protect it?

So what can we do to get our children back in touch with nature? Well, for a start I hope you, and any children you know, will use this book to get out and experience the wonders of the natural world for yourself. This isn't hard—there are many things you can do in any backyard, or even in a town or city park. There are things you can do as a family, or that your children can do on their own or with their friends. And there are organized activities, too, which are best enjoyed in the company of a knowledgeable expert.

I've arranged the activities into seasons, along with a substantial section of things you can do all year round. I've tried to be as specific as possible. If you already know how to climb a tree, then you can skip the directions, but if it's the first time your children are attempting it, there are step-by-step instructions on the best way to do so.

To help you identify the animals and plants you see, I've included identification guides to common species, beautifully illustrated by some of our finest wildlife artists. And there are poems, fascinating facts, and snippets of folklore to keep you and your children entertained.

At the end of the book there are contact details of organizations, website addresses, and a selection of books to help you extend your and your children's knowledge of America's wonderful natural heritage.

So please don't put *The Bumper Book of Nature* away on a bookshelf and let it gather dust. This is a book to be used. Take it outdoors and get muddy fingerprints on its pages. It is, I hope, a book for life—something you can enjoy with your children as they grow up, and which they may perhaps even use one day to introduce their own children to wildlife.

I am a very lucky man. When I was a child, I learned to explore the world around my home. I walked under blue suburban skies, built dens in the scrubby woods behind our house, played around the local gravel pits—and because of all this I developed a love of nature. In later life, I became one of those very fortunate people whose lifetime's passion is also their job, as the producer of television nature programs. I owe all this to one simple thing: when I was growing up I was given the freedom that so many parents now deny their own children.

So now I want you to close your eyes and imagine a world where sending your child out into the natural world is a matter of course rather than a special event. And instead of preprogramming their every move and organizing their every moment, you give them one simple instruction: "Just enjoy yourself!"

xii

A note to children

If someone has given you this book, they must know that you are interested in nature—in birds and bees, foxes and frogs, and many other wonderful wild creatures.

But when was the last time you went outside and discovered nature for yourself—on your own or with your friends? Never? Maybe your parents are worried that you'll hurt yourself, or get dirty. Maybe you don't know where to go, or what to do, or how to tell what bird or flower you are looking at.

That's where *The Bumper Book of Nature* comes in. This book is packed full of exciting things to do—on your own, with friends, or with grown-ups. You can build a den, catch tadpoles, or pick blackberries. You can do something simple, like lie down in the long grass and look up at the sky, or a bit trickier, like keeping caterpillars and watching them turn into butterflies. You can do these things in your backyard, down at the local park, on a hike in the woods, or by the seaside, and in spring, summer, fall, and winter. Whatever the time of year, and whatever the weather, there's always something to see and do in the wild world!

To help you know what you are looking at, there are pictures of common animals and birds, plants and insects—so if you find a strange butterfly in your backyard, or see an unusual bird on the park pond, you can find out what it's called. And at the end of the book there's loads of useful information—websites, books, and organizations you can join to help you make the most of your interest in nature.

So I hope you won't just put this book away on your bedroom shelf and forget about it. This is a book you need to use, to take outdoors—even to get dirty! Make sure you ask a grown-up before you do any of the activities here; and if they want to come with you, that's fine. But as you get older and more confident, ask them if you can go out with your friends and enjoy the natural world on your own.

And if, like me, you fall in love with nature, I can promise you that you'll never be bored again—because there's always something to see, to do, and to enjoy.

Have fun!

xiii

All Year Round

The great thing about the natural world is that it never stops. Whatever the time of year, something interesting is going on; you just need to go out and discover it.

This book is arranged season by season, since there are many things that you can do only at a particular time of year, like listening to birdsong at dawn, watching butterflies, roasting chestnuts, or building a snowman.

But there are also quite a few things that you can do more or less any time of year, such as building a den, making a nature table, and climbing a tree. You can play hide-and-seek or go for a walk in the woods; skim stones across a lake or feed your backyard birds; look for mammal tracks or start keeping a nature diary—or all of these things.

So there's no excuse, because whatever the time of year, the natural world is out there just waiting for you to explore it!

Build a den

When I was growing up, one of my favorite pastimes was making a den in the woods at the back of our house. I say woods, but this was really just a narrow strip of trees and scrub between the bottom of our garden and the back road. But to us it was "the forest," and we spent many a happy hour creating cozy hideaways out of bits of wood and old rugs we found in the garage. A few years later, the trees were all chopped down, and our adventure playground vanished forever.

Do you remember, when you were very young, pulling all the cushions off the chairs and divans and piling them up to make yourself a little hideaway, where no one could find you?

To make a secret place all your own it's even better if you can build a den outdoors—using fallen branches, bits of wood, and old bits of carpet instead of your mom's furniture.

Making a good den that will withstand gales and storms involves planning, construction, and teamwork. So join forces with your friends or brothers and sisters and make it a project that you can all enjoy—a much better way to spend a weekend or holidays than sitting in front of a TV or computer! It's also great fun.

Here are some tips on how to make a really good den

* You can make a den out of almost anything—natural or man-made—just as long as you can make walls and a roof, creating an enclosed space where you can hide away from the outside world.
* Keep it simple: larger bits of wood—either planks or fallen branches—will help you build a structure that you can cover with a quilt or rug to create a roof.
* Think about what you are trying to do: maybe draw a quick sketch on a bit of paper to show your friends.
* Listen to other people's advice—they may be able to improve on your design.
* Once you've got everything you need to build your den, start making the walls from the bottom up.
* When you've got the basic structure, cover it with a piece of material, such as an old sheet, blanket, rug, or remnant of carpet—and *not* your mom's best quilt! If the material you use is waterproof, a plastic painter's tarp, for example, so much the better—it will help keep the inside snug and dry.
* Then cover your den with smaller and lighter leafy branches to create a camouflage canopy—but don't forget to leave a gap large enough for a door!

* Bring another piece of material, or old blanket, to lay on the floor of the den to make it really comfortable.
* Once it's complete, stand back and admire your creation—your den is ready to be occupied.
* Bring along some food and drink and have an indoor picnic, outdoors.
* And once you've built your den, sit quietly inside and see what's going on outside—a den can make an excellent hideout for nature watching. . . .

And a few more tips

* A really quick-and-easy way to make a den is to hang a length of clothesline between two tree trunks or branches, tied fast at either end, and then just drape an old sheet or quilt over the top. Secure the edges with heavy stones or bits of wood, and hey, presto! An instant den.
* For very young children, simply hang a quilt or rug over the backs of chairs and put a rug inside for them to sit on.

Make a nature table

Back in the 1950s, 1960s, and 1970s, many elementary schools had a nature table, where children could bring in items they had found on the weekends, or discovered on nature walks with their classmates.

Nature tables are the ideal way to mark the passing of the seasons and to get to know about the incredible variety of natural objects you can collect.

Misguided fears about children coming to harm have more or less brought an end to this wonderful way of learning about the natural world. But there's no law against nature tables, and with a bit of common sense any potential hazards can be identified and removed. So why not start one yourself—at home or at school?

Things you can collect for your nature table

* Anything that falls off a tree: pinecones, dried leaves, acorns, nuts and seeds, berries, fruit, whole twigs, or small branches that have blown off in the wind.
* Pieces of tree bark you find on the ground.
* Dry thistle heads, seedpods, grasses, little clumps of moss or lichens.
* Flowers, which you can either keep in a jam jar full of water or press to dry and preserve them. (See pages 150–152.)
* Inanimate objects: stones, pebbles, and rocks—look out for unusual shapes or colors.
* Birds' feathers—from pigeons, gulls, crows, hawks, and smaller birds. Look out for real gems, like the gorgeous blue feathers of a blue jay, or the red feathers of a cardinal.
* Shells: either from the beach, or if you don't get to visit the seaside, from the snails and other creatures in your garden.
* Dead stuff—such as beetles (whose hard exoskeleton means they last a long time), spiders, or delicate skulls of birds.
* Old birds' nests (the nests are old, not the birds).
* Mushrooms and toadstools—just as long as you use rubber gloves and wash your hands carefully after you handle them.

You can also put field guides on display to help you identify what you find. (See pages 254–256 for details.)

Tip

To make your nature table even more exciting, add a glass tank where you can keep creatures you've collected, such as frogs' eggs (which will turn into tadpoles, then into frogs), or caterpillars (which will turn into pupae, then into butterflies), as well as minibeasts, such as spiders, ants, and snails.

How to identify . . .
trees

Our grandparents' and great-grandparents' generations could put a name to most of the trees they would see on hikes out of town; but in the past few decades we seem to have lost this rich store of knowledge. Many people today on a walk through a forest are unable to tell which trees they are passing; this is a great pity, because once you can put a name to a tree you can also learn a lot more about it and the wild creatures that depend on it.

Trees are a wonderful aspect of the wild world. North America is home to the world's biggest, tallest, and oldest trees—750 species in all—and these mighty giants are as much a part of our natural heritage as bald eagles and grizzly bears. Indeed, given how many creatures depend on trees for their own survival, trees may be the most important living things on the continent.

To identify which tree you are looking at, it's best to use a range of different features. For some, like the oak and sycamore, the leaves are really distinctive; while for others, like the beech and elm, the overall shape of the tree also helps you. Buds, flowers, seeds and fruits, and the bark are also good ways of telling one tree from another.

How to identify . . .
trees

Sugar maple
The classic "maple syrup" plant (see page 238 for a recipe for maple syrup candy). Like other maples, the sugar maple's leaves are not alternate but paired opposite along the twig. Mainly grows on well-drained soils in the northeastern United States.

White oak
One of the most familiar of our sixty different kinds of oak, though mainly found from the eastern United States to the Midwest, the white oak is a common tree of woods, hillsides, and riverbanks. Its distinctive seeds are acorns. Produced in fall, they are a favorite food of many animals, including squirrels.

Quaking aspen
The most widely distributed tree in North America, found in dry woods across much of the United States, this member of the poplar family is a medium-size, fast-growing tree with small, heart-shaped leaves and pale, gray-green bark crossed with dark marks. Seeds and buds provide food for a wide range of creatures.

Eastern cottonwood
This member of the poplar family is found from the Rocky Mountains to the eastern United States, where it grows in low-lying areas near water known as bottomlands. Triangular leaves with coarse teeth, sticky buds, and, later in the summer, green pods produce fluffy, cottonlike seeds.

American sycamore
Widespread across the eastern and midwestern United States and south to Florida, this tall tree has very distinctive, broad leaves, round fruits, and a mottled bark, which often peels off in large flakes.

California redwood
Also known as the coast redwood, this magnificent tree—the tallest, and one of the oldest, living things in the world—can be found along a narrow strip along the Pacific Coast, where it thrives in moist, damp soil.

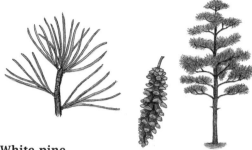

Douglas fir
Named after a nineteenth-century Scottish botanist and explorer, this huge and impressive conifer grows up the Pacific Coast and along the slopes of the Rocky Mountains. Has flat, yellowish green needles and hanging cones.

White pine
The two species of white pine, eastern and western, can be found in the cooler regions of North America, growing on sandy soils and in boggy areas. Needles come in groups of five.

Eastern red cedar
A member of the same family as junipers, this medium-size tree provides juicy, purple fruits that are a vital food for many different birds and mammals—and as a result it benefits by having its seeds spread.

American elm
Also known as the white elm, this tree grows to sixty feet tall, with a broad, spreading crown giving it a distinctive shape. Leaves are oval and pointed, with serrated edges; twigs are gray with chestnut-colored buds. Found mainly in the eastern United States to the Midwest. Sadly, this species is very susceptible to Dutch elm disease.

American beech
One of the iconic trees of the eastern forests, whose pale gray bark and paperlike leaves make it unmistakable. In fall it produces pods containing two or three triangular brown nuts, which are a much-needed winter food for many creatures.

10

Climb a tree

When was the last time you climbed a really good tree? Maybe you've been told not to climb trees because you might fall and hurt yourself. But what sort of a life is it if you never learn to take risks?

Actually, I'm a bit wary of climbing trees myself—but when I do so, I'm really glad I did. That's because tree climbing is a great way to learn the limits of your sense of adventure. It doesn't matter if you don't get all the way to the top—what's important is that you try your best and perhaps get a little bit farther each time.

* Late fall is the best time for climbing: once the leaves have fallen off it's easier to see what you're doing. But you can climb trees at any time of the year.

* Old jeans and a long-sleeved top are better than shorts and T-shirts, to prevent you from grazing your knees and elbows. Wear sneakers with a really strong grip, rather than sandals or boots.

* Choose the right sort of tree: large, old trees are best, since they have stronger branches and fewer twigs to get in the way.

* Dead trees are tempting to climb, but remember that their branches are more likely to snap.

* Take a few minutes to work out your route before you start climbing. Make sure your feet support the weight of your body, and that you always have at least one hand firmly gripping a branch.

* If you're not sure a branch is thick enough to support your weight, test it first by pulling hard with your free hand. And don't rush—that's the sure way to fall.

* Once you find a comfortable spot halfway up a tree, sit down on a branch and have a good look around. You're seeing the world in a different way from usual—from above. Spend a few minutes quietly looking and listening, and you'll be amazed at what you discover.

* Climbing down is actually more risky than going up: so once again, take your time, and make sure your feet and hands are in the right place each time you move, and that you have firm footing as you descend.

11

Hang upside down from the branch of a tree

Next time you're walking through the woods or a park, find a large, mature tree with a

thick, horizontal branch sticking out from the trunk (beech trees are particularly good for climbing), a couple of yards above the ground. Climb up to the branch; then carefully hook your legs over the branch and hang upside down from it. It's a whole new way of seeing a familiar world.

Make a rope swing from a tree

One of the most enjoyable things to do in your backyard or a local park is to make a rope swing. Because it can move in any direction, instead of just backward and forward like swings in a playground, a rope swing is much more fun!

You will need

* A length of high-quality rope about one to one and a half inches thick and long enough to reach from your chosen branch to the ground, plus another yard or so to be safe.
* A round disc of wood—perhaps an old chopping board, or a cross section through a tree trunk, large enough to sit on and thick enough to support your weight (at least one and a half inches, preferably thicker).
* Some sandpaper and a sanding block if you need to smooth the edges of the wood.
* A power drill.
* A ladder.
* A grown-up to help you with the power drill.

Find your tree

Choose a big, solid tree with a strong branch from which to hang your swing. Look for a mature, healthy specimen, such as an oak, with thick, horizontal branches at least a foot across. Select a branch growing between three and five yards above the ground. Check beneath where you plan to hang your swing to make sure the ground is reasonably level, and that there aren't any sharp objects such as tree stumps or big rocks that might hurt you if you fall off.

Now, make your swing

* Ask an adult to use the power drill, with a spade-style wood bit, to make a hole in the center of the piece of wood wide enough to thread your rope through it.
* Place the ladder securely against the branch, and make sure someone is holding it securely at the bottom. Then tie one end of the rope around the branch—ideally using a bowline knot, which will hold it secure. The bowline is one of the easiest and most effective of knots.
* Decide how high you want the seat (about one yard off the ground is best).
* Getting someone else to hold the seat in position, thread the rope through the hole in the center and tie a thick knot beneath the seat to hold the rope in place—you should tie at least three knots here.
* Give a firm tug before you start using it to make sure everything is secure.
* Then enjoy having a swing!

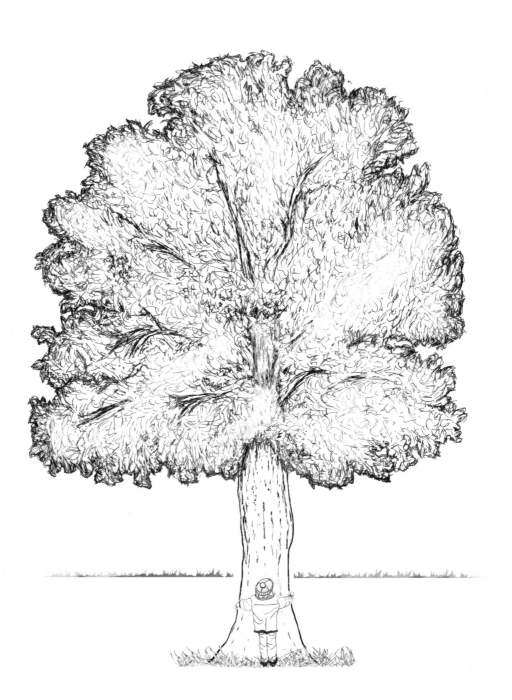

Tell the age of a tree

It's quite hard to tell the exact age of most living creatures. Once a baby bird has fledged and molted into its adult plumage it will look the same whether it's two or twenty years old. The same goes for other animals.

But one group of living things has made it a lot easier for us, at least once they've died. If you look at the cross section of a tree trunk, you can see a series of rings, each inside another, from the center to the edge. Each ring represents one year of that tree's life, so by counting them, you can work out how old that particular tree is.

But there's much more to tree rings than simply using them to work out the age of a tree. Scientists can measure the distance between each ring to work out whether or not a particular year was a good or bad one—a hot, dry summer, for example, will limit growth that year, producing a narrow gap between rings; while a warm, wet summer will allow the tree to grow faster, producing a wide one. This is known as *dendrochronology* and is used by scientists to measure climate change.

To count tree rings for yourself, you first need to find a dead tree, preferably one that has been felled so that either the trunk or its stump remains. Rings are counted from the center outward; the ones nearest the center are the oldest, and those closest to the bark are the most recent.

Most large felled trees will be between fifty and a hundred years old, but some large ones may be several hundred years of age.

But, can you tell the age of a living tree without cutting it down?

Yes, you can. Not quite as accurately as with a dead tree, but still close enough.

Using a tape measure, measure the girth (the distance around the tree) about one and a half to two yards above the ground. Then apply one of the following rules:

✳ If the tree is surrounded by lots of other trees (such that it has to compete with them for the sunlight needed to grow), every half an inch of girth equals a year's growth.

✳ If the tree is standing on its own, with plenty of access to sunlight, then every inch of girth equals a year's growth.

So a tree in a forest measuring about two yards around is over one hundred and fifty years old; while the same-size tree standing alone is only about eighty years old. A word of warning, though: some species grow more quickly than others; for instance, a pine tree or sycamore will usually be older than an oak of similar girth.

One of Earth's oldest trees is the bristlecone pine in the White Mountains of California, nicknamed "Methuselah," after the oldest man in the Bible. Methuselah—which, incidentally, is also Earth's oldest living thing—is more than 4,700 years old. That means it began growing almost 3,000 years before the birth of Christ, and at least a century before the building of the Great Pyramid at Giza in Egypt.

Make a bark rubbing

This is a good way to appreciate the patterns made by the bark of a tree, and it can also be used to identify different kinds of trees—though it's often easier to look at leaves and the general shape of a tree to tell what it is.

What to do

✳ Place a piece of plain white paper up against the bark of a large, mature tree.

❋ Using a pencil or crayon, rub firmly and evenly across the surface of the paper so that the pattern of the bark is revealed.

❋ Once you've made several different bark rubbings, lay them side by side so you can compare the different patterns made from different kinds of trees.

Tip

By using a large roll of plain white lining paper (which you can get from your local hardware or crafts store), you can use different colored crayons to make a continuous bark rubbing, which you can then use to wrap birthday and holiday gifts.

Listen to the heartbeat of a tree

Believe it or not, you can actually listen to a tree—an experience that really does give you a new way of understanding the living world.

All you need is a recording-and-listening device known as a contact microphone—the kind that musicians use to record the sound of individual instruments, such as a guitar or piano. They are not very expensive (between $15 and $75) and can be bought from most electronics or music stores. You may also want a pair of headphones to make it easier to listen.

You can either connect the microphone to an amplifier and speaker so you can listen to what is being picked up at the time, or plug it into any recording device such as a minidisc or even a video camcorder, and record the sound to listen to it later.

To listen to a tree, carefully place your contact microphone inside a hollow trunk, against its surface; plug it in, and wait. You should hear all sorts of strange sounds—most of which are made by tiny grubs nibbling away at the wood. Remember that you need to make sure the microphone is in direct contact with the tree or it won't work.

Tip

You can also use your contact microphone to listen to and record other natural sounds, such as those inside an ants' nest or even the inside of a compost heap. Again, make sure it is pressed up against the surface of whatever you are listening to.

How to identify . . .

common birds

Feeding our backyard birds has truly become a national pastime in recent years, with millions of dollars spent annually on
equipment and food designed to provide a five-star service for
the birds. But we benefit, too: feeding birds in our backyards
gives us the opportunity to get great close-up views, and often
leads to a wider interest in the birds of our neighborhood and
even farther afield.

You probably already know more birds than you think—most
people can identify a robin and a cardinal, a dove and a chickadee. The next step is to put a name to the species you are looking
at, and then start to learn more about their behavior and habits.
Soon you'll have turned into a full-fledged birder!

This is just a starter's guide to some of our common birds—
there are plenty more, so make sure you get hold of a field guide
to the birds of your area.

How to identify . . .
common birds

Black-capped chickadee

Small, neat, and cheeky, found in woods and backyards across much of North America, though not in the South. Black cap and throat contrast with white cheeks and pale brown flanks.

Mourning dove

A slender, elegant dove with a pale pinkish brown plumage, a long pointed tail edged with black and white, and black spots on the wings. Found throughout the United States, its hooting song is often mistaken for the call of an owl.

American robin

Surely our most familiar bird, and one of the best-loved birds of North America. Found throughout the continent, this large and sturdy thrush is often seen on grassy lawns. Combination of dark head, gray back, and reddish underparts make it unmistakable.

Ruby-throated hummingbird

The most common and widespread North American hummingbird, and the only one likely to be seen in the eastern United States. Adult males have a distinctive ruby red throat (white in the female); both male and female are green above, with white edges to their black tail.

Gray catbird

Related to mockingbirds, the catbird gets its name from its mewing call, often uttered from the depths of thick vegetation. Our only medium-size gray songbird, it also has a black cap and deep reddish brown under the long tail. Found in most states, though very rare on the West Coast.

Blue jay

One of the most familiar, colorful, and noisiest birds, especially in the eastern states, where it is a common bird of woods and backyards. Blue above, pale gray below, with a black "necklace," in flight it reveals white edges to the tail.

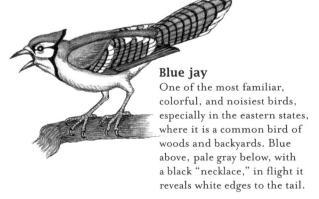

Northern mockingbird

Conspicuous and noisy, the mockingbird lives up to its name by mimicking a wide range of other songbirds in its extraordinary song. Long-tailed and mainly gray, with pale beneath and white wing bars. Most common in the southern and eastern United States.

European starling

This introduced species has thrived on this side of the Atlantic, spreading throughout North America since it was first brought here over a century ago. Its combination of yellow bill and dark plumage with paler spots is very distinctive. An accomplished mimic, able to reproduce man-made sounds such as cell phones as well as natural ones.

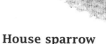

House sparrow

Like the European starling, house sparrows were brought here from Europe and have thrived in their new home. It took just sixty years to cross America from New York to California and it is now a familiar bird virtually everywhere we live, nesting in our homes in towns and cities throughout the country. Male's black throat is distinctive; female's drab and unassuming.

Song sparrow

Our commonest American sparrow, this plump, large-billed, and well-marked bird can be found throughout the continent, though its plumage varies greatly from east to west. Heavily streaked, with a distinctive spot in the center of its breast.

Red-winged blackbird

Almost certainly North America's commonest breeding bird. Loves to breed in marshy, damp areas but winters in a range of habitats, from towns to farmland, where it will form large flocks.

Northern cardinal

One of our brightest and most striking birds, its combination of crimson plumage, black face, and bright red crest make the male cardinal unmistakable. Mainly found in the East and the South, it is a regular visitor to backyards.

American goldfinch

With its striking custard yellow plumage contrasting with black on the head and wings, this is one of our most striking birds. Small and sociable, often feeding in flocks on seed heads.

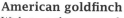

American crow

The commonest all-black crow in North America, found everywhere apart from the extreme Southwest. Large, sociable, and very intelligent, but like all crows tends to be unpopular with the public at large.

Look for owl pellets

David, the father of my old school friend
Daniel, recalls that when he was growing up during the 1940s and 1950s, he
and his friends would regularly dissect
owl pellets to reveal their contents.
Afterward, the challenge was to put
the various tiny body parts together
to create the skeleton of the owl's
prey—rather like assembling a
model airplane, but without the
instructions.

Owl pellets are incredible things. They look like small bundles
of gray fluff—until you start pulling them apart to reveal their
contents. For inside the furry outer layer you will find all sorts
of grisly objects: the bones and skull of whatever was the owl's
most recent meal. The owl swallows its prey whole but is unable
to digest the fur and bones, so it has to cough them up in a
pellet.

You will need

* A bucket of warm water.
* A pair of tweezers.
* A magnifying glass.

What to do

* The best place to look for owl pellets is on the ground beneath
  where the owl roosts by day: in either a large, mature tree or
  an old building.
* Scan the ground, searching for gray, furry-looking oval objects two or three inches long.
* Once you've found a pellet, the best way to open it up without

damaging the contents is to soak it in a bucket of warm water for an hour or so.

❋ Then, using the tweezers, gently tease it apart and pick out the clean skulls, vertebrae, and other bones.

The vast majority of owls' prey consists of small rodents, such as mice or voles. With practice (and by using a magnifying glass), you will soon be able to tell which body part, and sometimes which species, you are looking at. Individual bones such as vertebra, femur, and jawbone are fairly easy to identify, looking remarkably like miniature versions of our own.

There are almost twenty different kinds of owl in North America, ranging in size from the giant great gray owl—twenty-seven inches long and weighing over two pounds—to the diminutive elf owl. At less than six inches long and weighing just over an ounce, it is barely larger than a sparrow. One species, the burrowing owl of the southern United States, actually makes its nest underground!

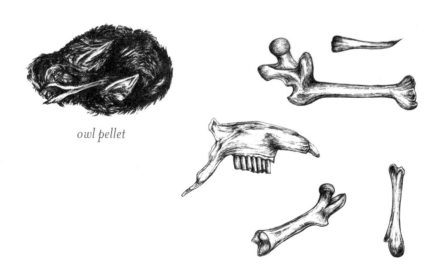

owl pellet

bone parts of small rodent

Look for mammal tracks and signs

We may have almost five hundred different kinds of mammals in North America, but how many do we regularly see? Not a lot—because many mammals are nocturnal, while others are so good at hiding from predators that they rarely show themselves.

The good news is that many mammals do leave signs of where they've been—if only we knew how to read them. So why not become a mammal detective, and see what you can discover?

What to look for

* Skulls and bones: when an animal dies, its flesh soon disappears, because it either decomposes or is eaten by another animal. But the skeleton—including the skull—is usually left untouched. With practice, you can pick out the telltale bleached white of bones. But remember, domestic animals like sheep and cows die, too, so you have to eliminate these first before you can be sure that your trophy comes from a truly wild animal.

* Antlers: in woods and other deer hot spots look out for shed antlers—especially toward the end of autumn, when the fighting males lose their antlers to conserve energy for the winter ahead. Antlers are amazing—one of the fastest-growing things in the natural world, they grow up to half an inch a day during peak season.

* Droppings or scat: not for the squeamish, droppings are actually one of the very best ways to detect the presence of a particular creature. We hardly ever see river otters, since they are mainly nocturnal, but it is quite easy to find their droppings, which are dark and tarlike, with a distinctive fishy smell.

* Tracks: footprints—left behind in soft mud or sand—are another good way to detect if a particular creature lives in your neighborhood.

* Hair: it's worth checking barbed-wire fences for bits of hair left behind as an animal squeezes through; for example,

front   *hind*

wood mouse

cat

raccoons often leave tufts of hair behind. Raccoon hairs have a black tip with a yellow band in front of a brown band before a white base. Opossum hairs are mostly white, though some brown shading may be apparent.

❋ Other signs: walk along a beach (especially just after autumn or winter gales) and you might come across the carcass of a marine mammal such as a dolphin, porpoise, or whale. Seeing the remains of these huge creatures at such close quarters always brings a mixture of wonder and sadness.

dog

Make a plaster cast of an animal track

One way to preserve what you find is to make a plaster cast of footprints or tracks made by passing mammals or birds. The best places to look for tracks are in soft mud around the edge of a pond, or in fresh snow.

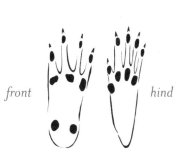

front *hind*

squirrel

fox

front *hind*

rabbit

deer

otter

front *hind*

weasel

You will need

* A soft brush (a large paintbrush is ideal).
* An eyedropper or pipette.
* Some small strips of wood or flexible plastic strip (to make a frame around the track and hold the plaster in).
* Plaster of Paris (bought from a craft shop or hardware store).
* A bucket or plastic container to mix the plaster.
* A stick or an old wooden spoon for mixing.

Making your plaster of Paris

* Add the plaster of Paris slowly to the water in the ratio of two parts plaster of Paris to five parts water.
* Mix it slowly, using a stick or old wooden spoon. **Warning:** *NEVER mix using your hands, as plaster of Paris can cause severe burns when in contact with skin.*
* When the plaster is roughly the consistency of whipped cream, it is ready to use.

How to make your plaster cast

* With the brush, carefully remove any bits of dirt or stones in and around the footprint.
* Using your eyedropper or pipette, suck up any water in the footprint—but be careful not to damage the outline of the print.
* Press your strips of wood or flexible plastic strip lightly into the earth, mud, or snow to make a frame around the footprint.
* Gently pour the plaster of Paris into the track until it reaches the same level as the surface of the mud or snow.
* Wait until the plaster is partly set (an hour or two), then remove the outer frame as carefully as you can.
* Wrap up the cast in some newspaper or bubble wrap, take it

mallard duck

home, and leave it in a cool, dry place to set properly (which usually takes a week or so).

* Once your cast is ready, you can paint it using poster paints and put it in a display with other casts—don't forget to label each one so you know which animal made it.

wood pigeon

crow

house sparrow

Grow mustard and cress

Growing mustard and cress on your kitchen windowsill is one of the best ways to watch how plants grow. The seeds sprout really quickly, and, what's more, you get something to eat at the end of it!

You will need

* A plate, saucer, or empty plastic strawberry container.
* Some paper towels.
* Mustard and cress seeds.

What to do

* Dampen about four or five pieces of folded paper towels (the absorbent kind) with water and place the pieces on a plate or saucer.

* Sprinkle the seeds on top of the paper.
* Every day or so, sprinkle water on top to keep the seeds damp.
* Then watch them grow.

Once your mustard and cress are ready (after two or three weeks), cut the leaves with scissors and serve sprinkled over a salad or mixed with hard-boiled egg and mayonnaise to make delicious egg-and-cress sandwiches.

Stand out in the rain

My grandmother firmly believed that getting caught in the rain was a surefire way to catch a cold, and in those days before central heating she was probably right. So to please grandmothers

everywhere, only do this when you're feeling fit as a fiddle, and have a warm, dry towel ready when you come inside.

As the lyrics of an old song say, "Remember—walking in the rain?" But when was the last time you deliberately went out in the rain—without an umbrella—and got wet?

Yet feeling the rain run down your face is one of the best ways to really feel alive. It doesn't have to be for long—just time enough to appreciate the sensation of pure rainwater, and to remember that without this stuff, there wouldn't be any nature to enjoy.

Sit or stand still for an hour, just watching and listening

If you are someone who likes to be on the move when watching wildlife, seeing new things all the time, this can be really tough. But you'll be amazed how different the natural world appears when you experience it from a single place over a period of time.

You can do this with or without binoculars—it's up to you. To be honest, I think it's better without, so you can really take in everything you see and hear. You can always have your binoculars handy in case you spot something really unusual.

It couldn't be simpler: just find a comfortable place, either sit or stand still for a whole hour, and see what turns up. Whether you're in your own backyard, a city park, in the middle of the woods, or on top of a mountain, I can guarantee you'll see or hear something different and new. I prefer doing this in a familiar place; it brings a completely new perspective to one's usual experience.

Pay special attention to what each creature is doing, and ask yourself questions. Is that the same robin I saw a few minutes ago, or a different one? What is that squirrel doing? How many butterflies can I see at once? Anything and everything is worth looking at—and when the time is finally up, you'll never look at a familiar place in quite the same way again.

Go for a "blind walk"

We talk about "wildlife-watching," but in fact a lot of the way we experience nature happens through other senses—especially hearing, smell, and touch. So why not try an experiment that will help you appreciate these different senses a bit more? Using a clean handkerchief or scarf, make a blindfold for yourself, and be sure you can't peek out the sides.

Then get someone you trust to guide you around a familiar place: your backyard, or a town or city park are ideal.

Start by standing still and listening. What can you hear? Depending on where you are, you may have to ignore the sounds of traffic or aircraft. If you're doing this in spring or summer, can you hear the birds singing? In summer, if you get close to some flowers, you may also be able to hear the buzz of insects.

What about smell? Again, ask your companion to guide you toward some flowers, and take a deep, long sniff. Different flowers have very different scents.

Next, try touch. Ask your guide to hand you natural objects: a leaf, a bit of bark, or a flower. Can you tell what it is just by feeling it? Check out its shape: you may even be able to identify particular leaves, or familiar objects such as berries, by touch alone.

If you feel a bit braver, get your guide to walk you around a larger area. Notice how the sounds and smells change, depending on where you are. You should be able to tell whether you are in light or shade—for example, if you walk under a large tree or into a forest clearing.

When you feel you've had enough, swap over and get your guide to do the same as you. This time watch how they notice things without using their sight. Are they having the same experiences as you or different ones?

And when you get home, write your impressions in your nature diary (see page 35), making sure you record how you felt, and remember what was different about doing without a sense we take for granted: our sight.

Play Poohsticks

Fans of A. A. Milne's Winnie-the-Pooh books will already be
familiar with this delightful game, which is easy to play and great
fun. You can do it on any bridge over a stream or small river—
just so long as the water flows underneath.

The rules are simple: each player finds a stick about a foot or
so long; then you all drop your sticks, at the same time, on the
upstream side of the bridge; run over to the other side to see
whose stick comes through first.

The game of Poohsticks first appeared in the book House at Pooh Corner, *published in 1928—though children have been playing similar games for centuries.*

Roll down a hill

Lie at the top of a dry, grassy slope (first making sure that there
are no nasty things you might hit on the way down), and start
rolling. If you want to stop, just stick your arms and legs out into
a star shape.

Feed the birds in your backyard

Millions of Americans regularly feed backyard birds—anything from throwing out a few leftovers from a meal to creating a five-star service station complete with designer foods and feeders. By doing so, we get a lot of pleasure from what is one of the best, and easiest, ways to get close to nature. It's best to avoid processed bread and uncooked rice, as these can be unhealthy for birds. Try whole grains, unprocessed bread, seeds, and nuts.

The great thing about feeding birds is that you get instant results. More or less whatever food you put out, within minutes a bird will come and take advantage of a free meal. And this is true whether you live in the back of beyond or in the middle of a city—birds are everywhere.

But if you really want to make a difference to your local birds, and get the most out of feeding them, you need to make a bit more of an effort. Here are ten top tips for feeding backyard birds.

1. Choose good-quality food. That means high-energy seeds such as sunflower hearts rather than peanuts. Sunflower hearts have a much higher oil content, which means the birds don't have to feed for so long to get the same amount of energy. In the short winter days, choosing sunflower hearts over peanuts will save many birds' lives.

2. Buy from a reputable supplier. Be careful about where you buy your food. Many garden centers and pet-food suppliers now stock good-quality food from leading bird-food companies, but others sell inferior stuff. If in doubt, get your food by mail order from one of the companies that advertise in birding and wildlife magazines.

3. Once you start feeding—don't stop. It's easy to be enthusiastic at the start, but when the first batch of food runs out, many people forget to order more, and the feeders run empty. That's the worst thing you can do, as your backyard birds will have begun to depend on you for food—so keep those feeders filled.

4. Feed birds all year round. We used to feed birds only during the winter months, when short days and harsh weather meant they needed extra food. But breeding birds and their chicks need energy just as much, so it's best to feed all year round. And you will see a greater variety of species as birds migrate during spring and fall.

5. Clean your feeders regularly. Dirty feeders, with rotting food, can easily spread disease, so give them a regular cleaning with soap and water, and remember to throw away any food that isn't eaten after a day or two.

6. Give birds live food. Birds love mealworms, which you can buy by mail order. Put them out in the breeding season, when both the adults and chicks need extra energy.

7. Just add water—with a birdbath. Birds want not only food, but also a place where they can drink and wash themselves. Birdbaths come in all shapes and sizes, from classic stone to modern plastic. Make sure that the sides of the bath are shallow enough for small birds to bathe safely, that you keep it filled, and that you clean it at least once a week to prevent disease.

8. Make your backyard bird-friendly. Providing birds with a self-service restaurant is just the start—you can attract a far greater range of species to your backyard by making it a five-star hotel as well. So don't forget birdhouses; and plant some native wildflowers, trees, and shrubs, which attract insects and provide a place where birds can roost at night.

33

9. Let a corner of your yard go wild—leaving the grass to grow and allowing wildflowers (what your mom and dad might call weeds!) to grow will attract insects, which in turn attract birds.

10. Keep a record of the birds you see. Keeping a notebook or diary of the different birds in your backyard—and noting any interesting behaviors—is part of the fun. Looking back in years to come, you'll be amazed at the variety of birds you've seen, and be able to enjoy recalling memories of what they were doing.

Note

Bird feeders often attract all sorts of other wild creatures to your backyard, such as squirrels, mice, and raccoons. And a word of warning: if you live in a neighborhood frequented by bears, DON'T feed the birds!

A small songbird, weighing maybe half an ounce or less, needs to eat about 40 percent of its body weight every day, just to survive. That's equivalent to a ten-year-old kid eating about 20 Thanksgiving dinners, 120 bowls of cornflakes, or more than 100 Hershey bars—every single day!

This recipe for an energy-giving "fat ball" for your backyard birds may not win any awards for culinary excellence, but the birds really love it.

What you need

* A large pan.
* Some lard or suet.
* Nuts, seeds, and raisins to add energy.
* A coconut shell, cut in two, with the flesh scraped out.
* Some string.
* An adult to help you with the drilling and cooking.

What to do

* Before you start, get an adult to drill a small hole in the top of one of the coconut shells and thread your string through, tying a knot to make it secure.
* Then ask them to warm the fat in a large saucepan over a low flame, being careful not to let it get too hot.
* Mix in the seeds, nuts, and raisins.
* As the fat starts to cool, pour the mixture into your half coconut shell until it reaches the top.
* Leave for an hour or two to harden—in the refrigerator if the weather is warm.
* Once it's hard, hang it up and wait for the birds to come.

Tip

If you can't get hold of a coconut, you can always use a large plastic or paper cup. Pierce a hole in the bottom of the cup, thread a piece of string through it, and fill the cup to the brim with the fat mixture.

Keep a nature notebook and diary

Once you start noticing different wildlife around you, you might want to keep a written diary of what you see. Over the years you'll find that your nature diaries form not just a record of your sightings, but also something you can look back over, to recall wonderful days out and about, or memorable encounters with wild creatures. I used to write down sightings in notebooks but now find it easier to type my records straight into the computer. But it doesn't matter how you keep your records, just make sure you do it in the first place.

Tips

* Always write down the key facts:
- Date (you can use a desk diary to make this easier)
- Location—for example, my garden, Central Park, the Grand Canyon, Cape May, N.J., etc.
- Time of sighting/time spent in the field
- Who you were with
- Weather conditions: sunny, cloudy, or wet? Approximate temperature, etc.
- Names of species you saw
- Any interesting or unusual behavior
- Memorable moments

It's a good idea to have two notebooks: a small, portable one to take out on walks, and a larger one to write up your sightings and experiences when you get home.

A handy alternative to a field notebook is a small, portable voice recorder—either a microcassette or a newer digital version. They save your fingers from getting cold and enable you to watch a bird or animal at the same time as recording what it's doing, but make sure you carry a spare set of batteries.

If you see something you can't identify, concentrate on getting the essentials down on paper or tape, such as what it looks like—making a quick sketch is a good way to do this. This is especially important if it's a bird; they often fly away before you've taken proper notes. When you get home you can look up the mystery creature in a field guide.

Remember, your nature diary doesn't have to be a record of visits to exotic or far-flung locations. The most rewarding diary you keep is likely to be the one of sightings in your own backyard or hometown.

Go for a walk in a graveyard

When it comes to looking for wild animals and plants, it's easy to overlook one of the best places of all—and one that can be found in most towns and cities in the country—a graveyard.

Because of their age (many Christian churches are several hundred years old), graveyards—even those in the center of a city—offer wildlife a real sanctuary.

From season to season, year to year, and century to century, graveyards have provided an undisturbed place where all God's creatures can find a home. Few other places in America have remained more or less unchanged for so long, creating a real community of flowers and birds, mammals and insects.

37

Things to look for in a graveyard

* Birds: foraging among the gravestones for insects; collecting berries from plants such as holly, ivy, and yew; or building their nests in tall trees. Graveyards are a favorite haunt of robins, thrushes, and warblers, especially during spring and fall migration periods.
* Mammals: raccoons, squirrels, and deer all enjoy the benefits of plenty of food and lack of disturbance.
* Night creatures: owls often favor graveyards. Bats, too, are often found here—quite literally nesting in church belfries.
* Wildflowers: many scarce wildflowers find sanctuary in graveyards.
* Butterflies: nectar-rich flowers attract all sorts of butterflies as well as other flying insects.
* Peace and quiet: graveyards are also a wonderful place to sit and appreciate the rich variety of wildlife we share this planet with—go on, try it sometime.

Lichens

Every graveyard in America—whether in the town or country—holds one other ancient secret. For in the midst of death, there is a very special form of life. . . .

There are things living here that you could quite easily overlook. And yet they're all around us: on the gravestones, on the trees, even on the walls of the graveyard itself. They're not plants, and they're not animals, and they have an amazing lifestyle. And thanks to their great age, they have an extraordinary story to tell. The name of these organisms? Lichens.

The funny thing about lichens is that although they are everywhere, they are so easily overlooked. That's partly because they blend in so well they almost seem to be part of the stones themselves.

What exactly are lichens? In your school biology lessons you learn about symbiosis: the working together of two organisms—plants or animals—for mutual benefit. That's exactly what lichens are—a combination of a fungus and an alga. And this partnership certainly does create something truly amazing.

* Some lichens have been in existence for more than a century.
* They are among the toughest organisms on the planet, able to cope with extremes of heat and cold that would kill off most other living things.
* They are a really good way of judging air quality; they hate pollution, but thrive in clean air.
* Lichens are used to make all sorts of things, including perfumes, litmus paper, and antibiotic drugs. In the past, they were often used to dye material in different colors.

A poem about graveyards

The most famous poem written about graveyards—and one of the best-loved poems in the English language—is Thomas Gray's

"Elegy Written in a Country Churchyard," published in 1751. Here are the first few verses:

The curfew tolls the knell of parting day,
The lowing herd winds slowly o'er the lea,
The ploughman homeward plods his weary way,
And leaves the world to darkness and to me.

Now fades the glimmering landscape on the sight,
And all the air a solemn stillness holds,
Save where the beetle wheels his droning flight,
And drowsy tinklings lull the distant folds.

Save that from yonder ivy-mantled tower
The moping owl does to the moon complain
Of such, as wand'ring near her secret bower,
Molest her ancient solitary reign.

Three ways to find which direction you are facing without using a compass . . .

Knowing which direction you are going in isn't just useful—it could save your life, if you are stuck up on a mountain in dense fog, for example. So if you're hiking out in the wilds, or exploring anywhere off the beaten track, it's vital to carry a proper compass.

But if you're just off for a walk in the woods, and you get lost, here are three useful ways to find out which direction you're going in without a compass:

1. Use your watch (during the day)

(Of course this method only works with an old-fashioned watch with proper hands—not a digital model!) Take your watch off and point the hour hand at the sun. Halfway between the end of the hour hand and twelve o'clock is due south. So at 8 A.M., the halfway point is 10 A.M.; while at 4 P.M., the halfway point is 2 P.M.

If it's a cloudy day and you can't see the sun, hold a pen, pencil, or small straight stick, upright on the watch dial. Unless it is really overcast this will cast a faint shadow, so you can work out where the sun is in the sky.

2. Use the stars (at night)

Find the brightest star in the sky—one that you can see easily. Using a stick, look along its length at the star, as if you're looking down the sight of a gun, and make sure you keep as steady as you can. Wait a minute or two for the star to move.

* If the star has moved left, you are looking north.
* If the star has moved right, you are looking south.
* If the star has moved up, you are looking east.
* If the star has moved down, you are looking west.

3. Use the "stick-and-shadow" method

(This only works on a sunny day and does take rather a long time.) Push a straight stick into the ground. Mark the end of the shadow it casts, using a small stone or rock, or by scratching a mark in the ground. Keep doing this every hour or so—the place where the shadow is shortest (that is, closest to the base of the stick) points to the north.

Go out into your backyard at night

What could be simpler than to go out into your backyard at night, when it's dark? But you'll be amazed at how different such a familiar place can seem when the sun goes down. . . .

* Choose a clear night with a full or nearly full moon.
* Take time getting your eyes used to the darkness, especially if you've just come from a house with all the lights on. One way is to turn out the lights indoors first so your eyes can get used to the darker conditions before you go outdoors.
* Don't just look—listen, too. Though your yard is usually quieter at night than during the day, you may hear nocturnal creatures such as owls hooting; and if you listen carefully enough you may even hear the scratchings of nighttime mammals, such as mice or raccoons.
* Using a compact flashlight, lift logs and stones and look under them—there's likely to be all sorts of insect activity going on.
* You can take a brighter flashlight if you want—but remember it might frighten away the creatures you want to see.
* And don't forget to look up at the stars and moon. . . .

In western states use a black light to see scorpions. Scorpions glow under the ultraviolet light created from a black light. But to avoid eye damage, don't look directly at the UV light! Instead put the black light bulb into a fluorescent tube, which will show scorpions up to two feet away from the light.

Time thunder and lightning to work out how far away a storm is

Next time there's a thunderstorm, here's a good way to work out how far away the center of the storm is, and whether or not it's moving toward or away from you. Using the second hand on your watch (or counting "one elephant, two elephant, three elephant . . ."), work out the time difference between seeing a flash of lightning and hearing the following clap of thunder.

Because light travels almost one million times faster than sound (about 186,000 miles per *second* as opposed to about 750 miles per *hour*), the sound of the thunder takes longer to get to us, even though the lightning and thunder happen at the same time. The difference between the speed of sound and the speed of light works out at about one mile every five seconds—so if you hear the thunderclap ten seconds after seeing the lightning flash, the storm is about two miles away.

43

Count the colors of a rainbow

Do you remember this song? "Red and yellow and pink and green, orange and purple and blue. . . ."

A lovely lyric, but unfortunately not a very accurate one! The true colors of the rainbow are actually red, orange, yellow, green, blue, indigo, and violet . . . the colors of the visible light spectrum.

Usually the red is on the upper (or outer) part of the rainbow and violet is on the lower (inner) part—but just occasionally a second rainbow is seen outside the first, with the order of the colors reversed.

We see rainbows when the sun is behind us and the rain is in front—the effect is caused by sunlight shining through moisture in the air.

A handy way to remember the order of the colors of the rainbow is the mnemonic Roy G. Biv, in which each letter represents one of the seven colors.

Skip stones across a lake or pond

One of the most addictive pastimes is to skip a stone across the surface of a river, pond, or lake and see how many times it bounces before losing momentum and sinking into the water. Another name for this game is "ducks and drakes." It takes a bit of practice, but here are a few tips on how to play. . . .

* Find a smooth, flat, oval-shaped stone—it will skip much better than a round or rough one.
* The stone should fit comfortably in the palm of your hand—any bigger and it will be hard to throw properly.
* Position yourself sideways to the body of water, and throw the stone as hard and fast as you can—speed is everything.
* Throw the stone at an angle of about twenty degrees to the water's surface (from about the height of your elbow).
* If you can, try to flick your wrist so that the stone is spinning as it leaves your hand—again, this will help maintain its momentum.
* Don't forget to count!

In 1992, on the Blanco River in Texas, Jerdone Coleman-McGhee achieved thirty-eight bounces with a single stone, setting a world record for skipping a stone across the surface of water. Then, in July 2007, Russell Byars of Pittsburgh, Pennsylvania, shattered this record by achieving an amazing fifty-one bounces—and he has the video of his feat to prove it!

Play hide-and-seek

You can play hide-and-seek anytime and anywhere, so long as there are at least three of you. There are all sorts of varieties, some simple, others complex—but my favorite involves a group of "hiders" trying to outwit the "seeker" and get back to base first.

The rules

* Decide the boundaries of the area where you're going to play—your yard, your local park, etc.
* Choose something to be your home base: this can be a park bench, large tree—anything that's obvious.
* Choose who is going to be the first "seeker."
* The seeker closes his or her eyes and counts to ten, twenty, or a hundred—depending on the age of the children playing the game and how far you want them to go.
* The "hiders" run away and hide.
* The seeker calls out, "Coming, ready or not!"
* He or she looks for the hiders as they try to make their way back to home base.
* If the seeker sees one of the hiders, he or she should chase and tag them—as soon as they're touched they also become a seeker, trying to find the other hiders.
* Whoever gets to home base first is the winner and will be the seeker in the next game, unless nobody gets back to base, in which case the winner is the last person caught. If the seeker doesn't catch any of the hiders, and they all get back to home base, he or she is the seeker again.

At the end of the game, there is a tradition that the seeker calls any players who are still hidden using the phrase "Olly Olly Oxen Free!" The origins of this bizarre custom are lost in the mists of time. . . .

Visit your local wildlife sanctuary

So many people I know would love to visit a wildlife sanctuary or refuge but never get around to doing so. Sometimes they just can't be bothered to make the effort, but usually it's because they are simply not sure what to expect.

They worry about things like whether they'll be wearing the right clothes, or carrying the right equipment, or know what to do when they get there. Do they need to bring binoculars or a field guide? Will they be able to get anything to eat and drink? How will they know what to look at?

As a result, they don't go at all, which is a real pity, as wildlife sanctuaries are not difficult places to visit. Here are a few tips:

* Your nearest sanctuary might be closer than you think: there are thousands of local ones across the country, with details available at your local library or on the Internet (just type in "local wildlife sanctuary" and your area into a search engine).
* Organizations such as your local Audubon Society or departments of environmental conservation also have refuges and visitor centers all over the country.
* Wear comfortable clothing—depending on the weather and season, you could wear jeans or shorts, a T-shirt or a fleece, a jacket or a coat, but make sure you have suitable shoes—rubber boots or shoes rather than sneakers if it's likely to be wet or muddy.
* If you don't have binoculars borrow a pair from a friend.

* If you're a real beginner—or even if you're not—sign up for a guided tour. Many larger sanctuaries run regular events led by friendly experts who will be able to point out what's worth looking at and help you identify it.
* Large sanctuaries also have visitor centers where you can buy drinks and snacks or sit down for a light meal, and shops selling everything from books to binoculars—and much more, often including displays teaching us more about the plants and animals found in the sanctuary.

North America's first wildlife refuge was established by President Theodore Roosevelt in March 1903. Pelican Island, on Florida's Atlantic coast, was given federal protection against hunters, to safeguard the thousands of brown pelicans, herons, and egrets nesting there. Just over a century later, there are well over 500 National Wildlife Refuges covering a total area of almost 100 million acres, or about 150,000 square miles.

Become a conservation volunteer

Once you have become a real wildlife enthusiast—and hopefully you will be one after reading this book—you may want to give something back to the wild creatures you enjoy watching so much, or to the places you love visiting.

One way to do this is to become a conservation volunteer, working on weekends or in your spare time to help conserve or improve wildlife habitats. This is ideal for older teenagers or families.

Volunteering can sound a bit daunting, or perhaps too much like hard work without much reward, but the reality is usually very different. Most people who volunteer find that not only do they give something back to nature, but they also get something out of it themselves.

This can be a practical benefit—many people working full-time in wildlife conservation started off as volunteers—or it may be something less tangible.

Volunteers often talk about some of the obvious benefits of volunteering: meeting new friends, getting out in the open air, and feeling fit and healthy are just a few. Plus you get to see some great wildlife, too!

Ways to volunteer

* Get in touch with one of the big conservation organizations such as your state Audubon Society or local wildlife sanctuary. These, and all sorts of community projects, are always looking for volunteers. You don't need to be an expert: just be keen, and willing and able to offer a few hours of work every week or month.
* Some conservation organizations also offer opportunities for participating in conservation weekends, or longer holidays, which are great ways to get involved.
* Ask your friends and their families if they do any volunteering. You may be surprised at how many people already do so.
* If you don't like the first place you try, don't give up! There are many different projects out there, so you won't necessarily find the perfect fit the first time around.
* Your high school, college, or parents' firm may already have a program that allows you to do some volunteering. If they don't, maybe you can persuade them to help you start one.

Use nature to forecast the weather

Red sky at night, sailor's delight,
Red sky in the morning, sailors take warning.

This saying isn't just a quaint piece of folklore; it is also surprisingly accurate. That's because when clouds are tinged red by the setting sun, it means that the air to the west (where much of our weather comes from) is dry. This generally means the next day's weather will be fine.

But if the morning sky in the east is red, stormy weather is usually on the way. This saying is so well established it can be found in Shakespeare and in the New Testament, and it is accurate roughly seven times out of ten, which is almost as good as a professional weather forecaster.

This is just one example of our ancestors using natural events to try to predict the weather, for the next day, month, or whole season. Remember, they didn't have TV or radio weather forecasters, and it was vitally important that they knew what the weather was likely to do in the coming harvest season, or winter, for example.

Some of these techniques are more accurate than others, but all are worth knowing, since they can help you understand the way the natural world is affected by the weather.

So here are a few examples of how you can use your observations of the skies, plants, and animals to try to tell what the weather is going to be like. There are seasonal examples later in the book, but here are some more general ones.

✳ The calls and songs of several birds are supposed to indicate rain is on the way. Woodpeckers are sometimes known as "rain birds" because their calls are said to herald the coming of rain.
✳ Another sound that is meant to foretell rain is the call of the common loon, one of whose folk names is "call-up-a-storm." The Thompson Indians of western Canada believed that if a human being imitated the loon's haunting call, rain would come.

* The early arrival of geese in autumn, to some parts of the United States, has long been said to foretell a hard winter to come. In fact, birds migrate depending on local weather conditions, and they are no better at long-term weather forecasting than we are.

* Farmyard animals such as cows and sheep are also sensitive to changes in the weather. Cows are supposed to lie down when rain is on the way, while sheep become friskier or turn their backs to the wind.

* Take a close look at the moon, especially a new moon. According to folklore, if the points at each end of the new moon are turned up, a dry month will follow; if they are turned down, it will be a wet one.

* The color of the moon is also supposed to help us tell the weather—at least according to ancient folklore. A pale moon means rain or snow; a red or orange moon means stormy weather; and a strong, white moon means fine weather, especially in winter, because a strong moon is often a result of clear skies, which means fine weather at this time of year.

The direction of the wind is often supposed to indicate the coming weather: broadly, wet from the west, warm from the south, cold from the east, and dry from the north. But as one rather cynical verse says:

> *The south wind always brings wet weather.*
> *The north wind wet and cold together;*
> *The west wind always brings us rain,*
> *The east wind blows it back again!*

For local weather forecasts, based on more than two centuries of records collected since 1792, and all sorts of other odds and ends about America's weather, check out the *Old Farmer's Almanac*. This traditional publication is now available online at www.almanac.com. Another fine source of weather lore is the American Folklore Society, founded in 1888, which publishes a monthly magazine packed with great folklore stories.

Spring

Nothing is so beautiful as spring—
When weeds, in wheels, shoot long and lovely and lush;
Thrush's eggs look little low heavens, and thrush
Through the echoing timber does so rinse and wring
The ear, it strikes like lightnings to hear him sing.

—GERARD MANLEY HOPKINS

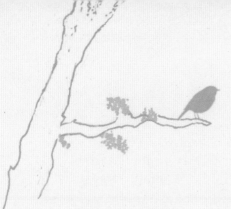

We all get excited about the coming of spring, don't we? That's because no other season packs quite so much activity into such a short time. Birds are singing, frogs spawning, flowers coming into bloom—and that's just the start. Later on there are baby birds clamoring to be fed, meadows filled with wildflowers, and everywhere you look the sheer exuberance of life—what the great Welsh poet Dylan Thomas called "the force that through the green fuse drives the flower."

Nature's version of spring is a bit more flexible than ours. We usually think of the season starting when the clocks "spring forward" at the end of March—just after the spring equinox—and ending on Midsummer Day, toward the end of June.

But all this activity couldn't possibly fit into just three months. So the birds in your backyard may start singing on fine days in February, while a mild spell might bring out the first bees and butterflies. By April some birds have already raised their first brood of young and are starting on another.

At the other end of the scale, migrating songbirds and shore-birds on their way north are still funneling through coastal hot spots such as Cape May, New Jersey, and Creek State Park, Ohio, in the middle of May. And birds keep nesting, flowers keep blooming, and insects keep buzzing all the way through the summer, making the end of spring quite hard to pinpoint.

The funny thing about spring is that though it does go on for a long time, certain key activities are tied to particular windows of opportunity. Miss them and you'll have to wait a whole year for another chance.

Look for catkins

My grandmother was born on February 11, 1901, and until she died at the age of ninety, our family would always give her a bunch of pussy willow catkins on her birthday. Pussy willow catkins are one of the first signs of life to appear in spring, often when there is still snow on the ground, but it was only years afterward that I discovered why. Because their pollen is carried by the wind, they need to appear before the leaves are on the trees, to enable the pollen to travel as far as possible.

Catkins are remarkable things—clusters of tiny flowers, either sticking up like a furry berry (pussy willow) or hanging down like a rather droopy-looking caterpillar (alder and birch). They are often found in the damper parts of woods, especially alongside rivers or streams, where the moist soil and slightly milder winter climate enable them to grow.

Catkins are either male or female—though the same tree will frequently have both. They begin to form in the previous autumn or winter and then emerge early in the spring—often appearing well before any other signs of life such as buds, leaves, or flowers.

pussy willow   *hazel*

Unlike other flowers, catkins don't have large, brightly colored petals because they have no need to attract insects to spread their pollen. Instead, they rely on one of the oldest and most reliable forces of nature—the wind.

The best time to find catkins is in February and March. Take a walk through the woods or a forest, especially one with a river or stream running alongside, and look out for them hanging from the branches.

To have a chance of pollinating successfully, catkin-bearing trees produce vast amounts of pollen—a single catkin may have as many as five million grains.

Listen for woodpeckers drumming

On a warm, fine day in early spring, listen for the drumming of woodpeckers. The best places to hear them are where there are plenty of large, old trees. Depending on where you live, you may hear up to half a dozen of North America's twenty or so wood-pecker species, ranging in size from the tiny downy (just over six inches long) to the giant pileated woodpecker (a whopping sixteen inches long). Sadly, the even larger ivory-billed wood-pecker, which once haunted the swamps of the southeastern United States, is now almost certainly extinct.

Just like birdsong, the drumming of male woodpeckers is for two reasons: to defend their territory against rival males, and to attract a mate. From early spring onward, the male selects a suitable tree (usually a hollow branch or trunk of a dead or dying one) and then proceeds to drum—producing up to forty blows every second. Just try drumming your fingers at that speed!

You might think that woodpeckers would get a headache from banging their beak against a tree—the equivalent of you or me repeatedly hitting our heads against a wall at more than fifteen miles per hour—but in fact they are superbly adapted to do so.

Woodpeckers have a thick skull, and their brains are very tightly packed inside to reduce the effects of shaking. They also have spongy tissue around their beak, which acts like an auto-mobile's shock absorbers, again minimizing the effects of the banging. The eyes are carefully protected and are closed just before the beak hits the tree to avoid being damaged by flying bits of bark.

So why don't woodpeckers fall off the tree when they drum? Because they have stiff tail feathers, which they wedge against the tree trunk or branch to keep them in place, used together with two strong grasping feet, which with the tail make for a strong triangular brace.

Once you've heard a woodpecker drumming, the next step is to try to see it. The earlier in the year you are looking, with fewer leaves on the trees, the better your chances.

But remember that woodpeckers are shy birds, and that their drumming can carry a long way. So try to approach slowly and quietly, until you're sure you're close to the drumming tree.

Then take a stick and beat a rapid rhythm on the tree trunk, as if you were trying to reproduce the woodpecker's own sound. With luck the bird will stop drumming and come to investigate what he thinks is a rival male intruding into his territory.

Once you've had a good view, don't confuse the poor guy by beating the stick again; he needs to get back to drumming to keep hold of his territory.

The acorn woodpecker, found in coastal forests all along the Pacific seaboard of the United States, has one of the most fascinating methods of storing food of any bird. Each autumn the woodpeckers bore holes in trees, then collect acorns and jam them inside, wedging the nuts in so they don't fall out. Later on, when the winter brings ice and snow and finding food is difficult, they have a ready-made larder!

How to identify . . .

birds of prey

Birds of prey—eagles, vultures, hawks, falcons, and owls among them—are some of the most fascinating and impressive birds in North America. Some live in remote parts of the continent; others have moved into our cities to live and hunt alongside us, providing daily spectacles for office workers!

In fall, birders gather at watch points all across North America to witness one of the most spectacular of all bird migrations—the "hawk flight"—as species that breed in the north of the continent head southward for the winter. The following spring, the same watch points see the passage north to breed.

Owls—the other group of hunters—are mainly nocturnal, secretive, and often hard to see, though some species do hunt at dawn and dusk.

Whichever species you are watching, it is hard not to be impressed by the sheer power of these masters of the hunt.

How to identify . . .
birds of prey

Rough-legged hawk

A bird of the far north, although in autumn they head south from Canada to winter across the United States. Like all buteos, they can be variable in plumage, but distinctive long wings and dark upperparts contrast with a white rump.

Turkey vulture

Popularly known as turkey buzzards, these birds are part of nature's cleanup squad, expertly scavenging the remains of dead animals, and in doing so performing a valuable service to our ecosystem as a whole. Their distinctive dark plumage and red skin on the head and face make them easy to identify. Found throughout the United States, though in winter they move south.

Broad-winged hawk

Smallest buteo, found mainly in the eastern United States. Can either appear very pale below or show contrast between dark head and body and paler underwings. Pointed wings and a long tail create distinctive silhouette. Large flocks, or "kettles," of these birds can number in the thousands during fall migration.

Sharp-shinned hawk

Our smallest true hawk, not much bigger than a kestrel, but with distinctive rounded wings, small head, and long tail, often fanned out in flight. Found throughout the United States, and often seen on migration in spring and fall.

Northern harrier

Slender and elegant, with long, narrow wings and a long, slender tail, which give it a very buoyant flight action very different from other birds of prey. Males pale gray; females and juveniles brown with a distinctive narrow white rump.

Red-tailed hawk

The commonest and most widespread buteo, the red-tailed hawk comes in a bewildering range of plumages, ranging from dark brown to almost white below. Adults show the distinctive red tail. Common throughout the United States, with one famous pair breeding on an apartment building off Central Park, New York City!

Bald eagle

Symbol of the United States, and rivaling the golden eagle as our largest bird of prey, this noble-looking bird is mainly a scavenger, often found near water. Once declined almost to the point of extinction in some areas, it has now made an impressive comeback. Adults show distinctive yellow bill and white head and tail; juveniles all-brown.

Peregrine falcon

The fastest creature on the planet, the peregrine falcon (its name means "wanderer") is a truly awesome sight, especially when hunting, when it can swoop down onto an unsuspecting pigeon at almost two hundred miles per hour. Once declined almost to extinction because of pesticides, it has now made an impressive comeback.

Barn owl

One of the most distinctive North American owls, its pale plumage, heart-shaped face, and floating flight make it easy to identify. Usually found in more open country than other owls, where it hunts for mice and voles. More common in southern states.

Osprey

Also known as the fish hawk, this distinctive bird of prey is found near water throughout the United States. Easily identified by its very pale underparts and dark mask across the eye. In flight it may appear gull-like in shape and color.

Great horned owl

Common and widespread throughout the United States, yet like all owls can be hard to see—your best chance is to locate one roosting at dusk. Large, with distinctive ear tufts and staring yellow eyes.

American kestrel

Small and slender, this tiny falcon is one of our most attractive birds of prey. Males show combination of rufous and blue-gray streaked with black; females mainly rufous-brown. Often hovers when hunting.

Burrowing owl

This delightful little owl can often be seen by day as it emerges from its underground burrow and stands up on its long legs. Mainly found in the South and West, especially in sandy areas.

Find the first spring flowers

What better way to welcome the coming of spring than to take a walk through your local park and look for the very first wildflowers of the season?

Exactly when you should do this depends on where you live: spring moves up the country gradually from the south, so the farther north you live, the later it will arrive in your neck of the woods. Local climate can make a difference, too: plants at higher elevations come into bloom several weeks later than those in the valleys.

Many of the flowers we associate with spring are in fact escapees from our backyard. Snowdrops, crocuses, and daffodils were all brought to North America by the early settlers, homesick for the native flowers of Britain and Europe. These tough little plants soon spread into the wild and now thrive in a range of habitats across the continent. Incidentally, the scientific name for snowdrop, *Galanthus nivalis,* translates as "milk-colored flower blooming in winter"!

The various species of violet are also early bloomers, usually appearing in March or April and gone by May or June.

Although it is sometimes frowned upon, there is no harm in picking a small posy of these early-spring flowers to take home and remind you of your walk in the woods. But never dig up a plant by its roots or pick too many flowers.

The name of another spring flower brought to the New World from the Old, primrose, derives from the Latin prima rosa—*meaning "first rose" or "first flower."*

Some recipes using spring flowers and plants

Many of us are understandably a little reluctant to pick and eat wild plants, fearing that we might fall ill. Yet our ancestors weren't so squeamish—they knew that harvesting, cooking, and eating wildflowers and plants was a great way to get good, wholesome food—and all for free!

Nowadays, sadly, the idea of collecting, cooking, and eating wild plants and other natural things like fungi has pretty much gone out of fashion—buying from the local store seems so much easier. People are also worried—unduly, I think—about the risk of poisoning themselves.

Of course you need to take care and make absolutely sure that you know what you've picked before you eat it. But it's well worth it for the thrill of knowing that you've gone out and foraged for yourself.

Here are a few suggestions for spring food for free

* Hawthorn: hawthorn leaves can be added to salads or cheese sandwiches, or just munched as you go on a hike. The very early bright green buds have a wonderful nutty flavor, and the later darker green leaves taste a bit like parsley.
* Stinging nettles: young shoots picked in the spring can be prepared in the same way as spinach or similar greens or made into a tasty and nutritious soup—with lots of iron and as much vitamin C as spinach. But wear gloves to pick them—they sting until they've been cooked.
* Wild sorrel: this slightly bitter herb, and its larger relative, wild dock, adds a lemony flavor to cooking and goes well with fish dishes.

* Burdock: the leaves can be peeled and used in salads, while the roots are also edible if baked or boiled. They can also be boiled up with dandelion roots to make a refreshing summer drink similar to root beer.
* Honeysuckle and nasturtiums: pick honeysuckle or nasturtium flowers and suck the nectar from the base—delicious! Nasturtium flowers are also great for adding color and a sweetish flavor to spring salads.
* Sassafras leaves: if you're feeling thirsty when on a hike in the wilds, chewing sassafras leaves is a great way to get your saliva flowing again!

One of the most abundant sources of food from the wild is the fronds of young ferns known as "fiddlehead ferns"—the curled-up, pale greenish yellow tops that appear at the bottom of a fern plant in early spring. These need to be cooked before eating to remove an unpleasant-tasting chemical. Fiddlehead ferns—mainly ostrich and cinnamon ferns—have traditionally been harvested and eaten in New England and eastern Canada, but they can be found across much of the United States. Bracken, a type of fern that is widespread, is best avoided, as it can contain cancer-causing chemicals.

To cook fiddlehead ferns

* Take off the brownish outer skin of the fern.
* Steam or boil the inner parts twice; use fresh water for the second boil. As with all vegetables, steaming retains more of the flavor and texture.
* Cook them for twenty minutes if steaming, ten if boiling.

Go see displays of cherry blossoms

In the cultures of the Far East—especially Japan and China—the annual appearance of the cherry blossom is a major cultural and social event, marked by a public holiday and celebrations in the streets.

Why not mark the coming of spring in your own neighborhood by taking time to enjoy cherry blossoms yourself? The streets of many of our towns and cities—notably New York City, Washington, D.C., Philadelphia, and Los Angeles—are filled with the wonderful sight and scent of flowering cherry trees, many of them originally given as a gift to the American people by the Japanese. The timing of the appearance of the flowers varies from place to place and year to year, but they usually bloom in March or April, marking the welcome change from winter to spring.

Many U.S. cities hold annual celebrations to coincide with the appearance of the cherry blossom each spring, of which the biggest is the National Cherry Blossom Festival in Washington, D.C., which takes place over two weeks from late March to early April and attracts more than 700,000 visitors each year.

Look for squirrel dreys

Wildflowers aren't the only things that are easier to see before the leaves are on the trees. Squirrel dreys—the equivalent of a bird's nest—are also easier to spot at this time of year.

A squirrel's drey is an untidy structure built high up in a tree. It's about the size of a large football and is made of twigs and lined with grass, bark, and moss. Unlike birds' nests, the twigs often still have the leaves attached, giving the drey its rather messy appearance. A drey also has a roof, whereas birds' nests don't.

If you're not sure whether what you've found is a drey or a bird's nest, it's worth waiting awhile. On warm, sunny spring days the squirrels will usually be active, and after a while you should see them coming and going to and from the drey.

On a fine day you may also see signs of courtship, as one or more males chase the female up and down the trees or along the ground. Once they've mated, the female squirrel carries the babies for about six weeks, giving birth later in the spring. She usually has about three cubs but can have as many as nine.

Squirrels are fascinating animals, and they are often the only furry wild animal that most city kids will ever see. Watching them as they climb acrobatically around the branches of trees or scamper up a trunk is always good fun.

Like other rodents, squirrels must constantly sharpen their teeth to enable them to feed. This habit has resulted in major power outages, when a squirrel has accidentally gnawed through a high-voltage cable. Sadly, in addition to the inconvenience this causes us, such actions usually result in the untimely death of the squirrel.

Listen to the dawn chorus

It's the best free sound show in the world—yet most people have never even heard it. That's because the dawn chorus starts well before most of us get up—roughly an hour before sunrise. In late spring, the peak time for birdsong can be as early as four in the morning.

But believe me, if you make the effort to get out of bed, you'll experience something you'll never forget—a whole orchestra of birds, each singing its heart out.

We may think the birds are singing just for us, but the truth is even more interesting. These are all male birds, and for them, singing is a way of life. They're defending their territory against rival males and at the same time trying to impress the local females.

So when you hear a bird burst into song, what he's really saying is "Hey! This is my space—so get out!" or "Hello, sweetheart . . . I'm ready for love—are you?"

If you want to enjoy the dawn chorus for yourself, here's what you need to know

* The peak time for birdsong is late April to mid-May, so that's the best time to be out and about. But some birds also sing from mid-February to the end of June, so anytime in this period is OK.
* Check sunrise times (using a diary or the Internet).
* If you can, choose a still, clear, and fine morning—birdsong carries better when it's not windy. Birds do sing in the rain but you'll get rather wet. . . .
* Birds sing everywhere—good places to hear them are your backyard or neighborhood park.
* Wrap up warmly—it can be very cold when you're simply standing.

- Take a hot drink and something to eat.
- Keep quiet—otherwise you won't hear what's going on.
- Don't worry about identifying every bird you can hear—just relax and enjoy the experience. Later, as the sun comes up, you can try to spot the birds and put a name to each songster.
- If you prefer to go with the experts, your local Audubon Society or bird club will run regular dawn-chorus walks—consult their websites for details.

And if you really can't be bothered to get up so early, just open your window before you go to sleep, add an extra quilt or blanket to keep you warm, and set your alarm for 4 A.M.—then enjoy the dawn chorus from the comfort of your bed.

More than nine hundred different kinds of bird have been recorded in the United States and Canada, of which more than half breed here. One of the most common is the red-winged blackbird, with an estimated population of almost two hundred million.

Provide a home for purple martins

At almost eight inches long, the purple martin is the largest of North America's nine swallow species. With its large size and handsome, glossy, bluish purple plumage, this is one of our most popular birds—and a welcome sight as they return northward each spring to nest in our neighborhoods.

And when I say neighborhood, I mean exactly that! The whole of the eastern race of the purple martin now breeds in homes provided by us—specially designed birdhouses where colonies of these beautiful birds can nest and raise a family.

Purple martins return from their wintering grounds in northern South America from February in the southeastern states, to as late as May in Canada. So it's best to put up a house for them early in the year or during the autumn.

You can make a home yourself, but they are pretty complicated structures, so it's usually easier to buy a ready-made one. Prices range from less than $50 for a basic model to well over $500 for the larger and fancier versions. Which you choose is up to you and your budget—to be honest, the cheaper ones are just as good for the birds!

If you haven't already got purple martins nesting near your home you'll have to attract them. The best way to do this is to play tapes or CDs of their song, which will encourage newly arrived birds to come along and check out your neighborhood.

Soon they'll have moved in and started laying their clutch of between three and five eggs. These take about two weeks to hatch, and the youngsters stay in the nest for another three weeks before they take their first flight and begin to explore the big wide world.

Unfortunately, purple martins aren't the only bird to take advantage of the homes we provide. Two European species—the house sparrow and common starling—will enter a purple martin house, expel the owners (often killing the chicks), and take it over for themselves.

Tip

There are all sorts of tips on how best to attract martins to your home, including painting the boxes white to reflect the sun and keep the nestlings cool, adding guards to deter any predators, and even adding a little guardrail to stop the chicks from falling out!

The two western races of the purple martin prefer more natural homes; they often take over old woodpecker holes in Saguaro cacti!

Identify different birdsong

Getting to know bird songs and calls is a bit like learning a foreign language—apparently impossible at first, then daunting, and often confusing. No wonder so many people give up at the first hurdle, or don't even bother to start.

But unless you know at least a few sounds of common birds, you will miss out on so much—most experienced birders identify at least half the birds they hear on song or call—especially in spring, when birdsong is at its peak.

So here are a few tips about how to learn the sounds of our common birds—plus some useful mnemonics or memory aids to help you. Hopefully, you'll find that, just like learning a foreign language, once you have mastered the basics, things get a bit easier—and a lot more rewarding.

Tips

* Start in February or March, when the resident species are in full song, but before the summer migrants have returned—it's less confusing that way.
* Get outdoors early in the day—birds sing the most just before and after sunrise. Just before dusk falls is also a good time.
* Avoid areas with lots of noise from traffic or people.
* Listen first, and then try to track down the bird that's singing and put a name to it.
* Concentrate on three elements—pitch, rhythm, and tone:
  · Pitch: is it high or low?
  · Rhythm: is it fast or slow? Continuous or broken up into phrases? Repetitive or unpredictable?
  · Tone: is it happy or sad? Harsh or musical?

❋ Finally, once you have heard a bird and memorized its song, try to see it so you can confirm its identity.

You can also use mnemonics—words or phrases that sound like the song or call of a particular bird—to help learn and remember birdsong. Many of these are so well known that they have passed into our language, often in the very name of the bird itself. Here are a few to help you identify the birds you can hear:

❋ White-throated sparrow: "Old Sam Peabody, Peabody, Peabody"
❋ Barred owl: "Who cooks for you, who cooks for you all?"
❋ Black-capped chickadee: "Chick-a-dee-dee-dee"
❋ Northern cardinal: "Cheer-cheer-cheer"
❋ Mourning dove: "Hula-hoop-hoop-hoop"
❋ Ovenbird: "Teacher-teacher-teacher"
❋ American robin: "Cheerily, cheer up, cheerily"
❋ Red-eyed vireo: "Here I am, where are you, in the tree . . ."
❋ Tufted titmouse: "Peter-Peter-Peter"
❋ Carolina wren: "Tea-kettle, tea-kettle, tea-kettle"

The most persistent of all American songbirds must surely be the red-eyed vireo, one of which was observed singing its brief song-phrase a staggering 22,197 times in just ten hours—that's more than once every two seconds!

Take a close look in a pond

As kids, on fine days in spring, we would take our nets and jam jars down to the local stream, which we called the "watersplash," and look for whatever we could find. We weren't fussy—we'd collect everything from minnows to water boatmen, frogs' eggs to newts, and even the occasional leech. Beneath the surface of even the most ordinary bit of water there is a wondrous variety of hidden life.

We called it "pond dipping," and it is one of those activities that, although it takes a bit of effort to prepare for, really is worth it. Looking a dragonfly nymph straight in the eye, watching a pond skater as it whizzes across the surface, or catching your first fish is a truly wonderful experience.

When to go

Pond life really gets going in spring—though some creatures such as frogs begin their life cycle in January or February by laying their eggs, especially in the southern states. The best months are from April to June, when most creatures are at their peak of activity and the layer of algae that covers ponds later in the summer hasn't taken hold yet.

What to take

* A bucket or large plastic container (not glass, as it might break). Large empty ice cream tubs are really good, as you can see the creatures more easily against the white background.
* Galoshes or rubber boots if you don't want to get your feet wet. Or river sandals if you don't care!
* Fishing nets—one per each person.
* A magnifying glass to take a closer look at whatever you catch.

Tips

- Before you start, take a good look at your pond to see what's there—if you begin dipping too quickly you might frighten everything away.
- Put some clean water from the pond into your container.
- Start by sweeping your net as carefully as you can across the surface of the pond, the rim just beneath the water. This will scoop up any creatures that live on, or just below, the surface.
- Once you've done a couple of sweeps, turn the net inside out over the container. Try not to squash any of the creatures—some are very small and delicate.
- You can also dip your net deeper, to collect things like water snails, tadpoles, and perhaps a newt or dragonfly larva.

Now try to identify what you have caught. If you're really keen, lots of state and local wildlife organizations run pond-dipping events at their refuges. (See pages 252–253 for details.)

What to look for

- Fish: there are almost a thousand different kinds of freshwater fish in the United States, including gobies, minnows, darters, and sticklebacks.
- Amphibians: depending on the time of year, you may find frogs, newts, or salamanders at various stages of growth, tadpoles, or even eggs.
- Insects: on or just under the surface, look out for pond skaters (which use the surface tension of the water to support themselves), water boatmen, and various kinds of water beetle.
- Water snails: you should find lots of different kinds, in all sorts of shapes and colors.
- Shrimp: not pink (they only turn that color when they're cooked) but brown.

- Monsters: dragonfly nymphs are fearsome-looking creatures that will feast on any unfortunate creatures that stray into their territory.
- Nasties: watch out for leeches—the original bloodsuckers . . .

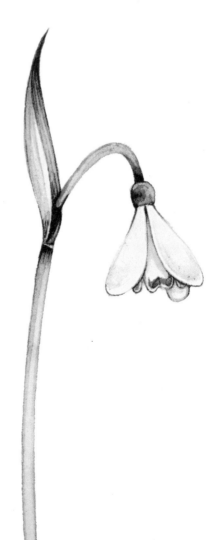

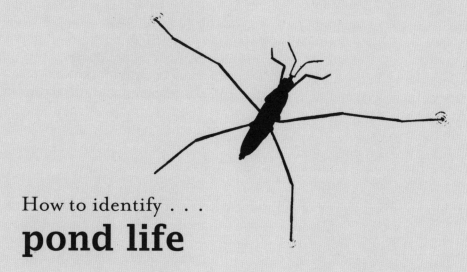

How to identify . . .
pond life

Dip beneath the surface of a pond and you'll be amazed at what
you find. Insects and their larvae, crustaceans, mollusks, and all
sorts of other creatures can be found here, and they can often be
caught easily using a net.

   Identifying them can be a full-time job, and the best way to do
so is to use a "key," which takes you through their features until
you eliminate all possible confusion species and arrive at the
right answer. But in the meantime, here is a guide to some of
the commoner freshwater creatures you are likely to find in our
lakes, ponds, and rivers.

How to identify . . .
pond life

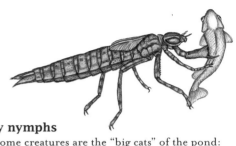

Dragonfly nymphs

These fearsome creatures are the "big cats" of the pond: ruthless and lethal predators able to seize and eat smaller creatures with ease. May be found either at the bottom of a pond or on plants. In spring and summer, watch out as they emerge from the water by climbing up a plant stem, spreading and drying their wings, and eventually flying off as an adult dragonfly.

Pond skaters

These bizarre little insects are able to use the surface tension of the water to support themselves, enabling them to "skate" from one place to another. Look for them on the surface of still ponds.

Caddis fly larvae

There are about a thousand different kinds of caddis fly in North America, ranging in size from about a quarter of an inch to just over one inch long. They begin their life as underwater larvae, often hiding beneath rocks, surrounded by a "case" of tiny stones and bits of debris, which they use to protect themselves. The adults are rather mothlike in appearance and live near ponds, lakes, and streams.

Water boatmen

These small, dark insects swim around in ponds, and occasionally in streams and brackish pools, looking for food, often tiny algae taken from the water or the mud at the bottom. They swim rather jerkily and also hold on to underwater plants.

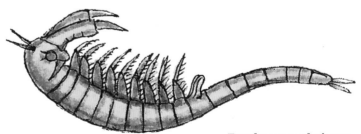

Freshwater shrimps

These tiny crustaceans prefer flowing water such as rivers or streams. They look very similar to the shrimps we find in rock pools at the sea.

Leeches

If you are pond dipping, this is the creature to avoid! Leeches attach themselves to the skin of fish (and human beings), pierce the flesh, and feed on blood. They come in a range of shapes, sizes, and colors but are generally broader at the rear end, tapering to a narrow head and mouth.

Pond snails

There are many aquatic varieties of snails living in our ponds, streams, and rivers, ranging from tiny species smaller than your fingernail to the giant pond snail, which grows to about the length of your thumb.

Whirligig beetles

As their name suggests, whirligig beetles tend to swim around on the surface of ponds, lakes, and streams, moving in a rather jerky, roundabout way. They have two pairs of eyes, enabling them to see above and below the surface at the same time—a useful technique when watching out for both food and enemies.

Backswimmers

Closely related to water boatmen, backswimmers swim around upside down, looking rather like a human doing the backstroke. They can often be seen at the surface of a pond, head beneath the water. Beware—unlike water boatmen, they can give a nasty nip.

Water scorpions

Named after their apparent resemblance to scorpions, though they are in fact related to water boatmen, back-swimmers, and other water bugs. They have forelegs specially adapted for grasping their prey, which they hunt underwater. Be careful when handling—they can bite!

Collect frogs' eggs—and watch them change into frogs

Have you ever wondered how a small ball of jelly with a black dot in the middle turns into a tadpole, then grows legs and arms and becomes a frog?

This truly is one of nature's miracles—and you can watch it happen.

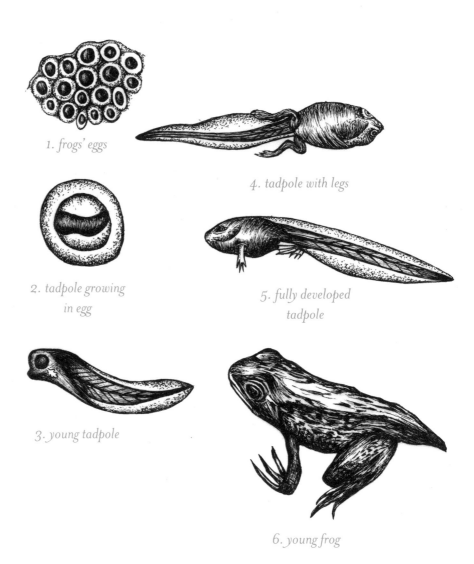

1. frogs' eggs

4. tadpole with legs

2. tadpole growing
in egg

5. fully developed
tadpole

3. young tadpole

6. young frog

You'll need

* A large glass jar.
* A fishing net (or your bare hands).
* A glass tank (at least eighteen by twelve inches).
* A pond or marshy area with some frogs' eggs in it (depending on where you live, frogs' eggs can be laid anytime between early spring and early fall).

Tips

* Most frogs breed after warm rains.
* Most frogs attach their eggs to branches or vegetation underwater.
* Choose a pond without many fish. Fish will feed on the tadpoles and adults, making it difficult to find frogs.
* Half fill your jar with water from the pond.
* Scoop up some eggs in your net or hands—making sure you don't squeeze them too hard. Always leave plenty of eggs in the pond to hatch naturally.
* Put the eggs in the jar and take it home.
* Carefully pour the frogs' eggs into your tank. (Make sure you've cleaned the tank with warm water first.)
* Fill the tank with a bucket of water from the same pond. Don't use tap water, as it's full of chemicals that may kill the tadpoles when they hatch.
* Put your tank somewhere cool and safe, such as a garage or shed; or, if you put a cover on it, outdoors.

Frogs' eggs take a week or so to hatch into tadpoles. Just like fish, tadpoles breathe through little holes in their sides called gills, and they swim as soon as they hatch.

You can feed your tadpoles on waterweed, but they also love chopped lettuce. Boil it for a few minutes to make it soft, and chop it up really small. Or you can buy goldfish food from the local pet store.

Don't feed them too much—and clear away any food they don't eat, otherwise it will become rotten and make the water smell.

Keep looking closely at your tadpoles as they get bigger. After about seven weeks you'll notice tiny bumps on their sides as their back legs start to appear.

A few days later, the same will happen at the front, and soon your tadpoles will have four legs and start to look a bit more like frogs.

At this point, put a rock or two into the tank, so the baby frogs will have something to climb onto as they grow.

Over the next week or so the tail will be reabsorbed into the body, getting smaller and smaller, and finally disappearing altogether. Your tadpoles have turned into froglets. Instead of breathing through gills, they are using their lungs—just like we do.

Now it's time to let them go—ideally in the same pond where you found the eggs in the first place.

By the way, it's easy to tell the difference between the eggs of frogs, toads, and newts. Frogs' eggs appear in familiar clumps of hundreds of eggs, often attached to branches that have fallen into the water; toads lay their eggs in long "strings," and newts just lay single eggs, which they hide beneath aquatic vegetation.

A typical frog will lay about two thousand eggs every year, of which only a tiny fraction will grow into adult frogs.

How to identify . . .
reptiles

This group is one of the most diverse of all the world's creatures and includes snakes, lizards, turtles, tortoises, and alligators, all of which display fascinating behaviors and are worth close study. Some, of course, are dangerous—even potentially fatal—so you should always take care when watching them, and never approach too close. But most reptiles will respect you just as long as you respect them, so make sure you do!

North America has a wide range of reptiles, including well over 100 different species of snakes, about 150 species of lizards, and more than 50 species of turtles and tortoises. Many live in the warmer South, yet the eastern and western states also have a good range of species.

Reptiles are "cold-blooded"—meaning that they need the sun's heat to warm up before they can become active—so they are best looked for early or late in the day, when they often bask in the sunshine in order to maximize their exposure to heat.

How to identify . . .
reptiles

Eastern garter snake

One of our most familiar snakes, this harmless creature is easily identified by its distinctive three yellow stripes running lengthwise down its body—one on the back and two on the sides. Found mainly in wet, marshy areas, often in towns and suburbs.

Diamondback rattlesnakes

The two species of diamondback rattlesnake—western and eastern—are the largest, and among the most dangerous, of all North American snakes, reaching six feet or more in length. Both are identified by their distinctive diamond-shaped pattern, and of course their fearsome rattle.

Corn snake

Also known as the red rat snake, due to its orange-red color and favorite prey. Color varies from place to place, enabling it to remain camouflaged. Prefers dry habitats, including farms and rocky hillsides.

King snake

The various species of king snakes are large, smooth-skinned snakes that constrict their prey. They vary in color and appearance, with the eastern king snake showing a distinctive white chainlike pattern on a dark background.

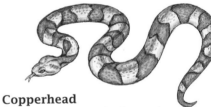

Copperhead

Like the cottonmouth, this is a large, venomous, orange-brown snake from the "pit viper" family. Contrasting body pattern and plain head. Found in forests and lowlands alike.

Cottonmouth

Also known as the water moccasin, this large, venomous snake lives in the swamps, streams, and ditches of the southeastern United States. It has a flat head and white gape (revealed when the snake is alarmed), and is brown with darker banding.

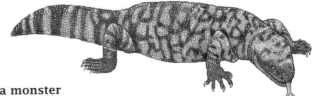

Gila monster

One of the world's only two venomous lizards, the Gila monster uses its venomous bite to fend off predators as well as kill its prey. A large, stocky lizard (up to two feet long) with an orange and black pattern on its back. Confined to the extreme southwestern United States.

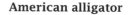

American alligator

The largest and one of the best-known North American reptiles, the alligator is a familiar sight in the swamps, marshes, and bayous of the southeastern states, especially Florida. Don't get too close—alligators can run faster than you can—at least when they are traveling in a straight line!

Box turtles

Eastern and western box turtle species are medium-size turtles (up to eight inches long) with a domed shell, intricately patterned in browns, blacks, and yellows. Is able to close its shell completely when threatened.

Gopher tortoise

As its name suggests, the gopher tortoise is an accomplished digger, using its powerful front claws to burrow into the soil, where it hides in a long tunnel. Large (up to fourteen inches), with a diamond pattern on the shell.

Common snapping turtle

A large turtle, as much as twenty inches long, with a big head, strong jaws, and a long tail. Lives in the muddy bottoms of ponds and swamps, mainly in the eastern half of the United States.

Desert horned lizard

Often known as the horny toad, because of its broad, flat shape and distinctive horns, this desert-dwelling lizard is native to western North America. Three to five inches long, they feed mainly on ants and other insects, often waiting near anthills for their prey to pass by.

Diamondback terrapin

A medium-size, gray turtle with a distinctive diamond-shaped pattern on the shell. Found in salt marshes and estuaries along the U.S. coast from Texas to Massachusetts.

Fence lizard

These typical lizards are commonly seen in prairies, woods, and other dry areas. They are gray-brown, with darker barring and a bluish patch on the throat and belly.

Go on an Easter egg hunt

Easter is one of the best times of year for getting out and about in your backyard or neighborhood park, or taking a hike through the woods. One way to make it a bit more fun is to organize an Easter egg hunt.

The rules are very simple. One person hides the eggs and works out clues to help the others (any number from two to twenty) to find them.

These clues can be in the form of a rhyme, for example:

An egg's an object without an edge,
So look for it in the backyard hedge . . .

Or a puzzle:

Clue: The next egg is hidden in a place that rhymes with marrow.
Answer: Wheelbarrow!

If you can't find an egg after a few minutes, ask for more clues. If you're really struggling, get them to say "Warm, warmer . . ." if you're getting close, or "Cold, colder . . ." if you're looking in the wrong place.

If there are younger children with you, make sure you let them find some of the eggs themselves, by giving them easier clues.

Like many Christian customs, giving eggs at Easter goes back beyond the birth of Christ to pagan times. Eggs are thought to symbolize the new life brought by spring.

Dye your Easter eggs yellow using flowers

A friend of mine tells me that when she was growing up she and her friends would collect saucepans full of flowers and boil them up with hen's eggs (not chocolate ones!) to make them turn a cheerful yellow.

This is her recipe

- Take a bucket or a large saucepan and fill it full of yellow flowers—dandelions and sunflowers, if they have sprouted, are ideal.
- When you get home, cover the petals with water, bring to a boil, and gently simmer for about ten minutes until the water turns yellow.

* Then add the eggs (if you can get hold of some, white ones are best, as they color better than brown), and boil for another ten minutes or so.
* Carefully remove the eggs from the saucepan, dry them off with a kitchen towel, and put them in an egg carton to cool.
* Once they are cool, use poster paints to decorate them.

And try these alternatives to yellow flowers for different colors

* Ripe blackberries (purple).
* Nettles (green).
* Beetroot (reddish purple).

Have a snail race

My mom was never a big fan of snails; in fact, she fought a running battle with them as they chomped and munched their way through her prized garden plants. But as I used to point out to her, snails do have their uses—if only as food to attract birds to our backyard. So if you take a more tolerant attitude, and don't mind a few leaves with holes in them, then snails are one of the most fascinating creatures.

Snail racing is something you can do anytime during spring or summer, when there are plenty of snails to be found in your yard or local park. It's a great thing to do with two or three friends.

* First, collect your snails—choose the largest ones you can find—and pop them in a bucket with a few lettuce or cabbage leaves to keep them going.

- Then you need to make a racetrack. Because snails can't be easily persuaded to go in one direction, the best way to do this is to get a large piece of wood, at least four feet across, with a smooth surface. Using a marker pen, draw a small circle in the center, and another, much larger, circle on the outer edges.
- When you are ready, put your snails in the center circle. Then just watch them go! Make sure you know which snail belongs to which person, so you can cheer your own one on.
- You can either have a time limit (say twenty or thirty minutes), after which the winning snail is the one farthest from the center circle, or just let the race go on until the winning snail has crossed the outer circle line.

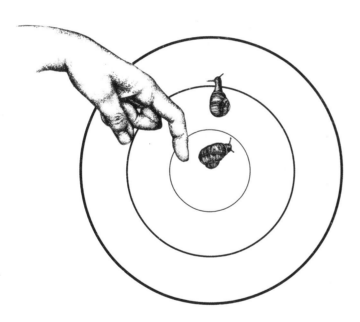

Another way to see how fast snails travel is to mark the shells of those in your backyard using Wite-Out (the stuff we used to use to correct typing errors in the days before computers) or colored nail polish. By marking individual snails with different patterns you should be able to identify which one has moved farthest in a single day or night—that's if you can find them again!

Snails are not known for their speed, but the speckled garden snail can move as much as 160 feet per hour. This is about 6,500 times slower than a Formula One racing car, and about 150 times slower than a human's walking pace.

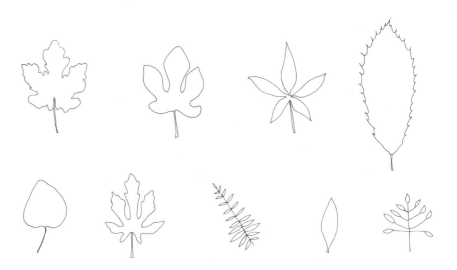

Identify trees by their leaves

Spring is a wonderful time to get to know trees. As they begin to leaf they adopt their familiar appearance and are generally easier to identify than at other times of the year.

The key place to start is by deciding what kind of leaf you're looking at. First try to work out if it comes from a broad-leaved tree, such as oak, maple, or sycamore, or a coniferous tree with needles, such as pine or fir. Then sort different leaves into shapes.

- Jagged: sycamore, red and black oaks, maples.
- Lobed: white oak, hawthorn.
- Heart-shaped: cottonwood, quaking aspen.
- Oval with pointed tip: American elm, alder, birch.

- Long and pointed: American chestnut, hickory, American beech, weeping willow.
- Slender needles: pines, spruces, larches, firs.

Why trees (and other plants) have leaves

- Trees need leaves to get their energy—by a process known as photosynthesis.
- It works like this: plants capture the energy from the sun using a substance in their leaves called chlorophyll (which also makes leaves green).
- They then combine it with carbon dioxide (from the air) and water (from the soil via the roots) to make glucose and oxygen.
- The plant can then convert the glucose into sucrose, and send it to the stem and leaves, or convert it into starch, to be stored for future use.
- The oxygen (a waste product from the plant's point of view) is excreted for us to breathe. Without this waste oxygen, animal life on the planet—including humans—could not survive.

Dig for earthworms

The humble earthworm must surely be the most underrated creature on the planet. Charles Darwin certainly thought so. He called them "nature's plow" and pointed out that without worms' ability to process decaying vegetation and get air into the soil, the world as we know it would not exist. As he said: "All the fertile areas of this planet have at least once passed through the bodies of earthworms."

Worms are vital to the health of the soil in your garden, and they also provide food for many creatures, including robins, moles, beetles, and even snails.

To dig them up, you'll need

* A small gardener's trowel.
* A plastic tray or box where you can put the worms.
* A magnifying glass.

The best time to look for earthworms is after a shower or longer spell of rain, when they'll come to the surface of the soil to feed, making them easier to find. But they won't stay aboveground for long; they are easy prey for birds, so you may need to dig in the soil to find them.

Use a small trowel, which allows you to turn over the soil gradually and find worms as you go, so you're less likely to damage them. If you do cut a worm in two it may be able to regenerate itself, but you should still avoid harming them if you can.

Once you've collected a few worms in a plastic tray or box, take a close look, using a magnifying glass. You'll notice that their body is made up of tiny rounded segments, joined together to allow the worm to move around by expanding and contracting its body. The front end is the one with the bigger segments making a bulge.

The earthworm's mouth is more or less invisible—but it does exist. As they eat, the food passes straight into their digestive system, where it decomposes and is passed out the other end.

There are about six thousand different kinds of earthworms in the world, one of which, found in Australia, can grow more than seven feet long. In a single acre of land there may be more than one million individual earthworms!

Look for mad March hares

The March hare . . . as this is May, it won't be raving mad—at least not so mad as it was in March.
—LEWIS CARROLL, *ALICE'S ADVENTURES IN WONDERLAND*

The brown (or European) hare is not a native North American species but was brought here by a German farmer living near Cambridge, Ontario, in the early twentieth century. Some of his hares escaped and soon spread southward into New England and other parts of the eastern United States, where it is sometimes confused with the native black-tailed jackrabbit.

Back in its native Europe the hare's courtship display has given rise to the saying "as mad as a March hare," made even more famous when the animal was immortalized by Lewis Carroll in *Alice's Adventures in Wonderland.*

In early spring, male hares (known as "jacks") start to get a bit frisky, and chase the females ("jills") around the fields, hoping to mate with them.

But the females don't give in so easily. They will often face up to their pursuer and try to fend him off. Sometimes the male and female will stand up on their hind legs and "box" each other with their front paws.

People were so baffled by this extraordinary behavior they assumed that hares went mad at this time of year—hence, the phrase "mad March hare."

Tips

* Early spring is the best time to search for hares; the grass is shorter, so they're easier to see. They are also a lot more active at this time of year.
* Like many mammals, hares are easiest to spot at dawn and dusk.
* Seek out traditionally farmed fields with short cropped grass, crops, or plowed earth, where the hares can run around.
* Scan the fields using binoculars—for such a large creature, hares can be surprisingly hard to see—and look for the black tips of their ears.
* Don't get too close or make any sudden movements; this will frighten the hares: either crouch down behind a hedge, or stay in the car—which makes an excellent hide!

How to tell a hare from a rabbit

* Hares are much larger, with longer ears that have black tips.
* When hares run, their longer legs are really obvious.
* Rabbits live in burrows; hares don't—though they will sometimes shelter in caves and rocky crevices.
* If they're boxing, they're hares!

Unlike rabbits, hares don't dig burrows. Instead, when they are alarmed or need to rest, they crouch down flat in little hollows in the ground known as "forms." The hare's apparent ability to vanish out of sight gave rise to the belief that the animal had magical powers.

Find a bird's nest

Egg-collecting is now against the law, and for very good reasons. Birds have enough problems to deal with in the breeding season without having to lay their clutch of eggs again because some person has raided their nest.

But the one good thing to be said about "birds nesting," as it used to be called, was that it gave you a really good understanding of what birds actually do in their day-to-day lives.

Finding birds' nests is not as easy as it sounds—most are hidden away in dense vegetation, to stop predators from finding the precious eggs or chicks—and learning how to spot them gave many older birders a really good apprenticeship in how to get to know various different species. Here are some tips on what to look for, when, and how.

Timing

* Most birds breed in spring—though in the bird world that can start as early as January and go on into late summer or even autumn.
* So the best time to look for nests is March or April—before the leaves on trees and bushes have had time to grow and hide them from view.
* Remember that some birds don't come back from their travels to Central or South America until April or even May—so don't look for warbler or swallow nests too early.

What to look for

* Not all nests are the same size and shape. Some, like those made by many songbirds, are neat, cup-shaped structures lined with grass or mud. Others, like crow's nests, are a rough assembly of sticks in the branches or twigs of a tree.

* Some birds, including chickadees and woodpeckers, nest out of sight in holes in trees—where they and their eggs and chicks can be safe from predators. Although you can't see the nest itself, you can sit and watch the birds flying in and out—especially once the chicks have hatched and the parents need to bring thousands of tiny bugs to feed them.
* Other birds make their nests in really unusual places. Odd nest sites have included a teapot, under the hood of a working tractor, and in a gardener's coat pocket.

How to find a nest

* Start by keeping your eyes open when you're on a walk or bike ride. Look at different levels—some birds like thrushes and wrens nest very low down in vegetation; others, like hawks, nest high in the top of a tree or on a cliff ledge.
* Another good way to find a nest—and to learn more about the bird and its habits—is to sit quietly in a suitable spot and watch the behavior of the birds you see.
* Look for birds carrying nesting material, such as grass, leaves, or twigs (early in the season) or food for chicks (later on).

* Some parent birds will also remove the chicks' droppings in a "fecal sac"—once memorably described as "shrink-wrapped poo."

Looking for nests on water

* Waterbirds, such as ducks, swans, grebes, and coots, often build their nest in full view, a few feet out into the water. To stop it floating away they attach it to an underwater plant.
* If the nest is close enough to the bank you should be able to see the eggs, and when the chicks hatch, you can watch them being fed by their parents.
* The chicks of most waterbirds are "precocial," which means they are able to swim—and to some extent fend for themselves—almost as soon as they hatch. But you can usually track them down by listening for the sound of tweeting as they anxiously call to remind their mom and dad that they're still here.

How you can help

* If you do find a bird's nest, be careful not to disturb it. Put any foliage you've moved back into position, and move away as quickly as possible so as not to attract the attention of predators or upset the parent birds.
* In spring, put out hair (of pets, horses, or humans) or bits of wool, straw, and grasses for the birds to use to line their nest.
* Make a birdhouse (see page 208).
* Put out live food, such as mealworms, to help parent birds feed their hungry young—especially in wet weather, when they need all the help they can get.

Many birds could not thrive in spring without the help of spiders. Not only do the spiders provide nutritious food for the adults and their chicks during the winter months, but spiderwebs are used in the construction of many species' nests.

Spring weather lore

Thanks to the movie *Groundhog Day*, starring that great deadpan comic Bill Murray, the whole world now knows about North America's famous natural weather forecaster, the groundhog—also known as the woodchuck, the largest North American member of the marmot family.

Legend has it that if on February 2, the groundhog sees its own shadow, then it will retreat back into its burrow. This is bad news: it means the winter weather will continue for a further four to six weeks. If, however, the skies are cloudy and there is no shadow, the groundhog will come out, signifying that spring is just around the corner.

This is based on the principle that high pressure, bringing sunshine (and therefore a shadow) foretells cold, stable conditions for the month ahead; whereas cloudy weather (and no shadow) means change is about to come.

There's only one tiny problem. Meteorologists have carefully studied what actually happens following the groundhog's annual appearance, and they have discovered that the appearance of a shadow, and the groundhog's subsequent behavior, make absolutely no difference to the timing of the coming of spring. Pity, as it's a great story—but at least it provides the excuse for a holiday!

Our ancestors had plenty of other proverbs and verses to help them predict the weather, often linked to religious festivals such as Lent, which are the forty days before Easter, and Easter. So it was said that:

Wherever the wind lies on Ash Wednesday, it continues during all Lent.

At the end of Lent, a similar forecast was made:

Rain on Good Friday foreshadows a fruitful year.

But another proverb is more ambiguous:

A good deal of rain upon Easter Day, gives a good crop of grass, but little good hay.

Other sayings were supposed to help predict the success or failure of the harvest, later in the year. So in Alabama, it was said that:

Fogs in April foretell a failure of the wheat crop.

Elsewhere, a more optimistic view was taken:

If by St. George's Day (April 23) the rye has grown high enough to hide a crow, a good harvest can be expected.

Saints' days like this were often used as markers by which to predict the weather and other natural events. So St. David's Day (March 1) is supposed to be a good day to sow oats and barley, presumably because the worst of the winter is over by then, while St. Patrick's Day (March 17) is meant to coincide with geese beginning to lay their eggs.

And it's hardly surprising that May Day—the main celebration of the coming of spring—gave rise to all sorts of sayings that try to forecast the weather for the season ahead. Several proverbs suggest that cold weather on May Day will bring a good harvest. This may well be true: after all, cold winters help to kill off molds, pests, and diseases—increasing the chances of a bumper crop.

Summer

Sumer is icumen in,
Lhude sing cuccu!
Groweth sed, and bloweth med,
And spring the wude nu . . .
—ANONYMOUS

"Summer is coming . . ." is the oldest known poem written in more or less modern English and shows our thirteenth-century ancestors' excitement at the arrival of the warmest, sunniest season of all.

Nowadays, summer is the ideal time to get out and about in the countryside, and enjoy the benefits of warm, sunny days and long, light evenings. But as the long summer vacation draws to a close and autumn begins, how many of us look back and realize we've missed the chance to enjoy all those classic summer pastimes for another year?

Here are dozens of things you can do during the summer months: from watching dragonflies to collecting caterpillars; city safaris to nights in your backyard; and a whole host of activities for a summer vacation at the coast.

So pack your shades, butterfly net, and binoculars, and get out there and enjoy!

Collect caterpillars and watch them change into butterflies

This is the best way for anyone to learn about the miracle of metamorphosis—one of the most complex and extraordinary processes in nature. And with a little effort you can see it happen before your very eyes. . . .

What you need

⦾ Something in which to collect the caterpillars: traditionally a large jam jar with a lid, but plastic food containers such as Tupperware boxes may be more practical. Remember to make small holes in the lid so the caterpillars can breathe.

⦾ Rubber gloves to pick up the caterpillars. Some caterpillars—especially the big hairy ones—have poisonous hairs (to make them unpleasant for birds to eat), which can irritate your skin.

Collecting your caterpillars

⦾ Look for caterpillars anytime between May and August, with the most variety available in June and July.

⦾ Once you find them, gather up a maximum of five and put them into your plastic container, ideally with a stem or two of the plant they are feeding on at the time.

⦾ When you collect the caterpillars, also bring home extra stems of the plant you find them on and keep them fresh in a jug of water. This is known as their "food plant," and many kinds of butterfly or moth caterpillars only feed on a single type.

⦾ Never pick up a caterpillar you find on the ground—it is searching for its food plant or wandering off to pupate and needs to be left alone.

Food plants of some North American butterflies

CATERPILLAR'S FOOD PLANT	BUTTERFLY GROUP
alder	tiger swallowtail
alfalfa	orange sulphur; blues (various species)
buckwheat	painted lady; blues (various)
burdock	painted lady
cabbages, broccoli, kale, and other brassicas	whites, including cabbage white
clovers	sulphurs
cottonwood	western tiger swallowtail; mourning cloak
docks and their relatives	coppers
elm	mourning cloak
grasses	California ringlet; skippers (various); satyrs (various)
hackberry	American snout; hackberry emperor
juniper	juniper hairstreak
lupine	blues (various)
marigold	dainty sulphur
milkweed	monarch; queen
mustard	cabbage white, Sara orange tip
nettles	anglewings (various), red admiral, painted lady
oaks	hairstreaks (various)
parsley	swallowtails (various)
passion flowers	zebra longwing; Gulf fritillary
shepherd's purse	orange tips (various)

snapdragon	common buckeye; variable checkerspot
sunflowers	American lady; painted lady
sycamore	western tiger swallowtail
thistles	painted lady
violets	fritillaries (various)
willows	western tiger swallowtail; mourning cloak

Looking after them

- Keep your caterpillars in a fish tank; you can buy one at any hardware or pet store. Put the stems of their food plant into a small jar of water inside the tank, and bring fresh plant material in every couple of days.
- Cover the tank with a lid to stop the caterpillars from escaping, but make sure there are enough air holes to keep them alive.
- It's best to keep your tank in a cool place, otherwise the butterflies will emerge too early—a basement or garage is ideal.
- Make sure you provide a good supply of the food plant as the caterpillars grow—they are voracious eaters. And the bigger they get, the more they eat; some caterpillars will need new supplies every day.
- From time to time your caterpillars will shed their skin and emerge looking fresh and new. You may notice bits of shed skin in the tank. When caterpillars change their skin they usually stay still. Make sure you don't pick them up at this time.

Pupation

Eventually your caterpillars will have grown to their full size, and at this time they are ready to enter the next stage of their metamorphosis—pupation.

In this incredible process, the caterpillar effectively goes into a state of suspended animation while its body is broken down into a kind of mush. It then reconstitutes itself into the next stage, the adult butterfly or moth.

Some caterpillars bury their pupae in damp earth, while others affix themselves to bark—so make sure your tank contains both earth and some old bits of bark, twigs, and branches to give them both options.

Pupae that form during the spring and summer generally hatch into butterflies or moths after a month or so; those that form in autumn usually remain in this state throughout the coming winter and emerge the following spring.

Emergence

When you think the adults are about to emerge it's a good idea to place some more twigs and stems in the tank so they can stretch their wings to dry them after they've come out. Don't be tempted to touch their wings at this stage, as you might damage them; just leave the insects alone and they'll sort themselves out.

Once they have emerged and the wings are fully dried and stretched, release the adults into the same area where you found the caterpillars. Watch out for birds, which can make an easy meal of a new butterfly. If possible, hide the insect beneath some foliage so it can't be easily spotted.

The word caterpillar *is thought to come from Old French via Middle English, and means "hairy cat." A typical caterpillar has more than four thousand muscles to enable it to move (we humans have a mere six hundred or so).*

104

Catch butterflies with a net

The early naturalists who pioneered the study of North American wildlife were more likely to carry a shotgun and a paintbrush than a butterfly net. Nevertheless, during the nineteenth century the British enthusiasm for collecting butterflies did cross the Atlantic, and the practice of collecting, killing, and displaying butterflies in cases became quite popular.

Nowadays we live in more enlightened times, and the collecting and killing of butterflies has, quite rightly, been discouraged. But there's nothing to stop you from using a butterfly net to catch them, so you can take a closer look before releasing them unharmed.

It's best to use a proper butterfly net, which can be bought from specialist dealers or on the Internet for a few dollars. These have fine mesh and are large enough for you to catch your quarry. You'll also need clear plastic boxes to hold the butterflies in (again, these can be bought from dealers), some with a built-in magnifying lens so you can get really close-up views.

Catching your butterflies

- Look for butterflies on a warm, sunny day, from about mid-morning until late afternoon, when they are most active. But be aware that during the middle of the day some butterflies may be a bit too active for you to catch them—they can fly faster than you can run!
- If there are plenty of nectar-rich flowers, your backyard is a good place to start. If not, visit a local park or forest, or a traditional meadow full of wildflowers.
- Check out areas where the sun and shade meet—butterflies often feed along flower borders and paths.
- Take time to get to know the habits of the butterfly you're chasing—some fly almost constantly, rarely settling; others will stay put for minutes on end, basking in the sunshine.
- Stalk your quarry. Butterflies are very sensitive to movement, so creep up on them slowly and carefully.
- Once you're within range (fewer than a couple of yards away), bring the net down rapidly on top of the butterfly, being careful not to bash it with the frame.
- You must get the butterfly in the tip of the net and then quickly fold the net over so it can't escape.

Once you've caught them

- Usually the caught butterfly will flutter its wings for a few seconds and then stay still. Carefully insert your collecting box under the rim of the net, and persuade the butterfly to enter. Be very careful not to damage its wings. Once the butterfly is safely in the box, slide the lid across to make it secure.
- Then take a few minutes to have a really close look. You'll see how the color on the wings changes, depending on the angle at which you're looking.

- With the help of a butterfly field guide you should be able to identify it—though with about seven hundred different species that can be found in North America (north of the Mexican border) this may take some time!
- After you've had a good look, release the butterfly in the same place you caught it.

Other ways to attract butterflies

- Place a white or yellow sheet on the ground in the sunshine, or drape it over bushes; this will often attract butterflies, especially early in the day when they need to warm up.
- Plant nectar-rich flowers such as honeysuckle, lavender, and lilac.
- Go wild—a patch of nettles in the corner of your yard is the ideal food plant for several different kinds of caterpillar.
- Put out rotten fruit—the juices will attract butterflies, especially on warm, sunny days in autumn when they are filling up on energy before the winter comes.

The monarch butterfly was thus named in the 1870s by the Boston entomologist Samuel Hubbard Scudder, because "it is the largest of our butterflies, and rules a vast domain." How vast a domain is truly mind-boggling: monarchs migrate hundreds of miles from the northern United States and Canada to Mexico and California, where they gather in the thousands to spend the winter in a milder climate. They sometimes go astray and have occasionally even managed to fly three thousand miles across the Atlantic Ocean, eventually arriving in the British Isles.

How to identify . . .

butterflies

Butterflies are some of our most beautiful and fascinating in-sects. Their life cycle, in which an egg hatches into a caterpillar, which itself turns into a chrysalis and finally emerges as a winged adult, is little short of a miracle.

They are also common (though sadly not as common as they used to be) and easy to spot—but on fine summer days they do fly a bit too fast for an observer to get a really close look. Catching them with a net and releasing them once you've taken a closer look (see page 104) is a great way to identify them.

There are about seven hundred different kinds of butterflies in North America, so a good field guide is essential if you want to identify every species you see. In the meantime here's a sam-pler of some of our commonest and most familiar butterflies.

How to identify . . .
butterflies

American copper
Found widely across the northern United States, this dainty little butterfly can be identified by its rich, copper color and dark spots on both the upper wings and underwings.

Monarch
The big daddy of North American butterflies, with an extraordinary life cycle, during which some butterflies travel hundreds—occasionally even thousands—of miles on their migratory journeys. Easily identified by its large size and distinctive black and orange markings.

Black swallowtail
The swallowtails are among our most elegant and beautiful butterflies, and the black swallowtail is one of the most striking, with a dark background set off by yellow markings. Widespread throughout the United States.

Cabbage white
The gardener's enemy is an alien species, accidentally imported from Europe, which has thrived due to its ability to feed on cabbages and their relatives. Today it can be found throughout the United States. White with dark edges to the forewings and a dark spot on each wing.

Clouded sulphur

A medium-size, custard yellow butterfly, with dark spots on the forewings, orange spots on the hind wings, and a black border surrounding the yellow. Confined to the northern and eastern United States, it is able to survive in a range of habitats, including tundra and mountaintops.

Variegated fritillary

Named after the checkered pattern on their wings, the fritillaries are among our most elegant butterflies. This large, orange and black butterfly has a direct flight but can be difficult to approach; it is found throughout most of North America.

Painted lady

This close relative of the red admiral is the most widely distributed butterfly in the world. It is another long-distance traveler, heading north each spring to breed in temperate latitudes throughout North America. Can be identified by its pale orange color, and black wing tips with white blotches.

Mourning cloak

This large and distinctive butterfly has dark wings edged with yellow, with a row of blue spots. It can be found in woods and forests throughout North America.

Red admiral

One of the commonest and most familiar butterflies of North America, the combination of black and white wing tips contrasting with orange-red makes the red admiral stand out from the crowd. An active migrant, reaching farther north than almost any other butterfly.

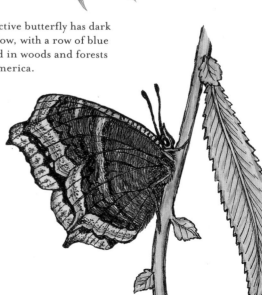

Go moth trapping

There are few creatures as misunderstood as moths. Normally sensible people go into hysterical panic when they come across one, or think that just because the larvae of a few species destroy clothing, all moths must be harmful.

The truth is that the ten thousand or more different kinds of moths found in North America (north of the Mexican border) are among our most varied, beautiful, and fascinating creatures, and the good news is that they are surprisingly easy to see. All you need is a way to attract them so you can get a closer look. . . .

There are all sorts of different ways to trap moths; some are cheap and simple, others a bit more complicated and expensive. But whichever method you choose, you are guaranteed more or less instant success.

You can either attract them with light, or tempt them with food. Several trapping methods take advantage of moths' love of sweet, sugary substances, including alcohol.

One theory as to why moths are attracted by bright lights is that they use the moon to navigate, so that when a light is switched on they try to orient themselves in relation to it.

But because the light is only a short distance away (as opposed to about a quarter of a million miles between Earth and the moon) the moth finds itself flying in ever decreasing circles until it hits the light. At this point its tiny brain assumes that the sun has come up, so it settles down to rest in the bottom of the trap.

When to trap moths

Moths are out and about virtually all year round, but the largest numbers and greatest range of species are on the wing in late spring, summer, and early autumn—and especially the months of June, July, and August.

Weather conditions play an important part: the best times for "mothing" are warm, humid nights with plenty of cloud cover and little or no wind. Although heavy rain will dampen their enthusiasm (and probably yours, too), a spot of light drizzle can encourage more moths.

Finally, don't bother using light traps on bright, moonlit nights, especially when there is a full moon, since they will be pretty ineffective.

How to do it

◎ Dusking: the simplest and quickest way to find moths is simply to search for them, using a bright flashlight and a butterfly net. The best places to look are nectar-rich plants where the moths will be feeding. Take a few small plastic containers with you to keep the moths in so you can get a good look at them later. Dusking works particularly well in the early evening when it is still light enough for you to see where you're going. It is also best early in the season—late winter to spring.

- Sheeting: similar to dusking, but done by shining a powerful flashlight onto an old white sheet. Within a minute or two the moths will start to arrive, and you can either examine them as they rest on the sheet or put them into the plastic containers for a closer look later.
- Sugaring: with an adult to help you, and using a large saucepan, mix together one cup of dark beer (a stout or porter works best), a tin (roughly sixteen ounces) of black molasses, and two pounds of dark brown (or muscovado) sugar. Bring to a boil, simmer for a few minutes (adding a shot or two of rum if you wish), then take the pan off the heat, and let it cool. Once the mixture is cold, transfer it into an old tin and use a paintbrush to smear it onto tree trunks, gateposts, or pieces of wood. Do remember that this will stain, so don't paint it on your backyard fence! Sugaring tends to work best early on in the night when most moths are active.
- Wine roping: use a similar recipe, but with red wine instead of beer, then soak lengths of rope in the mixture and hang them from the branches of trees.
- Outdoor lighting: many moths flutter to security and porch lights, so just switch them on and see what comes!

But if you're really keen on moth trapping, and don't mind spending a few hundred dollars (less if you share it among a group of you), then the best method is to use a full-scale "Robinson trap" or "Skinner trap," the latter named after a British pioneer of moth identification, Bernard Skinner.

These use a mercury vapor (MV) lightbulb, which gives out a very bright beam of ultraviolet light, which attracts the moths. You'll need an outdoor extension cable, since this will need to be plugged in at your house. And beware: *don't stare directly at the light; it could damage your eyesight.*

The moment you turn on the light, the bulb will begin to warm up, and within a few minutes the moths will start to arrive. Once they reach the light source they slip down the Perspex sides into the bottom of the trap. Here they find cardboard egg cartons where they can settle down unharmed until you come and check the trap, either later that night or early the next morning.

When you check your trap, be careful not to harm their wings as you remove the moths. You'll need a good moth identification guide, and a notebook to write down details of what you find. It's also a good idea to bring a digital camera to take pictures of the moths you catch, so you can identify them at leisure later on.

Once you've removed and inspected the moths, make sure you release them somewhere with plenty of vegetation to hide behind. And don't put them all in one place, since this will attract hungry birds.

If you live in a built-up area, make sure your bulb isn't visible from your neighbors' bedrooms, or the bright light may keep them up all night!

Moths have some of the most bizarre and delightful names of any of our wild creatures. These include: fall canker moth, green larch looper, false crocus geometer, hemlock angle, tulip-tree beauty, yellow-dusted cream moth, barred umber, royal walnut, pine devil, morning glory prominent, pandora pine moth, Griffin's sheep-moth, poplar tentmaker, modest sphinx, decorated owlet, bertha armyworm, and, my favorite, bicolored honey locust moth.

Watch damselflies and dragonflies

Dragonflies, and their close relatives the damselflies, are among the fastest, largest, most brightly colored, and all-around most impressive insects on Earth. Here are just a few amazing facts about them:

- Dragonflies have been around for over three hundred million years—tens of millions of years before dinosaurs appeared on Earth.
- They can fly at speeds of more than thirty miles per hour.

- Their eyes have up to thirty thousand different lenses.
- They are the tigers of the insect world: lone hunters, seizing, dispatching, and devouring their prey with ruthless efficiency.
- Despite their fearsome reputation, they do not normally bite human beings and cannot sting us either; but they do feed on other flying insects.
- Although they live for up to seven years, they spend almost all that time underwater in larval form; adult dragonflies stay on the wing for just a few weeks.
- With a body length of almost five inches, the giant darter is the largest of North America's three hundred or so dragonfly species. The smallest North American dragonfly, the elfin skimmer, is only about three-quarters of an inch long.

Our 130 or so different kinds of damselflies are generally smaller than dragonflies, but the best way to tell the difference is the way they sit when perched.

Dragonflies stick their wings out from their body, looking a bit like a World War I biplane (except the pairs of wings are one in front of the other rather than top and bottom). The smaller, more matchlike damselflies perch with their wings held along the length of their body, giving them a more streamlined appearance.

Different species appear at different times of year, with the earliest emerging on bright, sunny days in March or April, and the latest hanging around into the autumn. June, July, and August are the ideal months, and warm, dry days the best kind of weather. Dragonflies are unable to fly when it's raining or too cold.

In flight, it can be quite hard to see their colors, but as soon as a dragonfly or damselfly comes in to land it reveals its beauty. Different species can be identified by the colors and patterns of their head, thorax (the chunky area behind the head from which the wings stick out), and long abdomen.

As soon as they emerge, these insects are in a race against time to find a partner and breed, so that the female can lay the next generation of eggs beneath the surface of the water. Look out for two dragonflies or damselflies in a circular embrace as they mate.

Once the female has deposited her precious eggs, her parental duties are over: the eggs eventually hatch into tiny larvae, which feed voraciously underwater for several years.

During this period they shed their skin several times as they grow, before metamorphosing into the adult and emerging into the open air via a plant stem.

Tips

- Make sure your binoculars are able to focus at least as close as three or four yards (preferably even closer), which will allow you to get fabulous views of perched dragonflies and damselflies without disturbing them.
- A good way to work out which species you're looking at is to take digital photos, then look them up in an identification guide when you get home.
- Some dragonflies fly in a pattern along the edge of their territory, as they patrol its borders. Watch and you may be able to predict where the dragonfly will go next.

Dragonflies and damselflies have all sorts of folk names, many of them referring to their supposed ability to bite or sting, including horse stinger, adderbolt, and the devil's darning needle.

Give bumblebees a helping hand

It's sometimes said that it is scientifically impossible for a bumblebee to fly. Yet the bumblebee, seemingly unaware of this scientific "fact," manages to fly anyway.

And thank goodness it does. For without pollination carried out by the humble bumblebee, about one-sixth of all the food we eat would never be able to grow. Many of our wildflower meadows would never bloom. And our economy would lose out to the tune of an estimated three billion dollars a year. Some scientists even believe that if bees as a whole died out the human race would survive for only four more years before we, too, became extinct.

Other reasons to welcome bumblebees is that they are so beautiful—with their combinations of yellow, orange, black, and white—and often endangered, as a result of the overuse of agricultural chemicals. So anything we can do to give our forty-five different kinds of bumblebee a helping hand must be worthwhile.

Things to do

- Plant nectar-rich flowers—especially native species—in your backyard; the more you plant, the more bumblebees you will attract—and the better they will pollinate your plants.
- Make sure you have flowers in bloom throughout the year—bumblebees will often emerge on sunny days in winter to stock up on nectar.
- Stop using pesticides—they are just as harmful to friendly creatures like bumblebees as they are to less welcome ones.
- Don't panic if a bumblebee comes close—many don't have a sting at all, and even those that do are very unlikely to sting you.
- Put some bumblebee boxes in your flower beds—these are just like birdhouses but with two chambers, one for the queen and the other for the workers.

- Let part of your backyard grow wild, with longer grass and scrub where the bumblebees may also nest.
- Log piles are also great places for bumblebees.
- Finally, if you come across a hibernating bumblebee, try not to disturb it—emerging too early or in cold, wet weather may be fatal.

The myth that bumblebees can't fly goes back to the 1930s, when a British aeronautics engineer used a combination of the creature's size, weight, and wing length to work out that it could not possibly get airborne. What he overlooked was how the bumblebee flaps its wings—not up and down, like a bird, but in a complex figure eight—which when carried out two hundred times a second enables the bee to fly.

Take a really close look at an ant colony

Go to the ant, thou sluggard; consider her ways, and be wise.
—PROVERBS 6:6

What wonderful creatures ants are. Among the strongest (weight for weight), most intelligent, and sociable insects on Earth, they are endlessly fascinating to observe and study.

Ants live in underground colonies that are formed from a series of interconnected chambers, tunnels, and passageways with separate areas for storing food and looking after the eggs and young. These are created and maintained by thousands of "worker ants," wingless females, every one of which is at the service of the queen—the colony's pampered egg-laying machine.

You can watch ant colonies on a sunny day as the workers emerge and scatter in search of food to bring back underground.

Try catching a few ants in a plastic container and taking a close look through a magnifying glass. Notice that like all insects their bodies are divided into three parts: the head, thorax, and abdomen; they have two antennae attached to the head, and six legs emerging from the thorax.

Another way to get an insight into the lives of ants is to create your own colony, known as a "formicarium" or "ant farm." This allows you to see the tunnels and cavities created by the worker ants. You can either make your own—with two sheets of glass or Perspex sandwiched close together and filled with sand or soil—or buy one by mail order or online.

Some amazing ant facts

○ For every human being on Earth there are an estimated one *million* ants.
○ An ant has a highly developed sense of smell—at least as keen as a dog's and far better than ours.
○ Ants are, for their size, the strongest creatures on Earth: they are able to lift and carry objects weighing fifty times their own body weight.
○ There are between 12,000 and 14,000 species of ants in the world, of which about 700 different kinds live in North America.

The great American biologist E. O. Wilson turned his attention from studying birds to ants when he went blind in one eye as a result of a childhood accident. He remains fascinated by these amazing creatures: "Ants are the dominant insects. No matter where I go, no matter how different the human culture, no matter how different the natural environment, there are the ants."

How to identify . . .

bugs

Insects and other invertebrates—or, as we often call them, bugs,
creepy-crawlies, or minibeasts—are the most successful group
of creatures on the planet. They were here long before the dawn
of mammals, let alone human beings, and will still be here long
after we and our civilizations have gone. So they deserve a bit of
respect—they're not just pests to be squashed!

True insects are a huge group—well over one million species
worldwide, and close to ninety thousand in North America, out-
numbering birds by about a hundred to one! They are also a very
varied group—with beetles the most abundant, closely followed
by flies, and also bees, wasps, ants, termites, lice, grasshoppers,
crickets, cicadas, and ladybugs, as well as the larger, colorful,
and more noticeable butterflies, moths, and dragonflies.

Then there are all the other insectlike creatures that belong
to quite different groups: spiders, for example, and millipedes,
centipedes, and scorpions, to name but a few.

With so many different species in such varied groups it is
simply impossible to identify every species you come across. A
good field guide is essential if you want to learn more, but in the
meantime, here is an overview of some of the main insect and
invertebrate groups to get you started.

How to identify . . .
bugs

Bumblebees
These large, slow-moving, and hairy insects are some of the most important on Earth, as they pollinate many of the plants that provide us with food. Usually black and yellow, like other bees they live in social colonies centered on a queen.

Millipedes
Reputedly have a thousand legs, though in reality they have anywhere between forty and four hundred, arranged in pairs along the segments of their body. Slow moving, they prefer damp places and are often found under rotting wood or in soil.

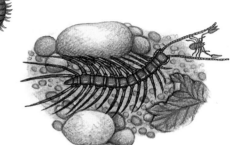

Centipedes
Like the millipedes, the number of legs on a centipede does not quite live up to its name—thirty or so is the usual count. All centipedes are predators, stunning their prey with venom from their two front claws.

Harvestmen
Closely related to spiders, and usually known as daddy longlegs, these have a small body and eight very long legs, giving them a delicate appearance. Often seen around the home and backyard.

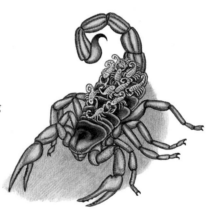

Scorpions
Often feared and avoided because of their nasty sting, scorpions are related to spiders and have four pairs of legs, which enable them to move very quickly in pursuit of their prey, which they kill with the sting held in their curved tail. Often found in deserts and drier environments.

American tarantula
One of the largest and most feared spiders in North America. Found in the southern states of the United States, the American tarantula is a large, hairy, brown spider that will rear up on its back legs if disturbed. However, they are relatively harmless to humans.

Dragonflies
Dragonflies are some of the largest and most spectacular insects on the planet—and also very successful, having been around since before the dinosaurs roamed the Earth. Larger species (true dragonflies) are voracious predators and perch with their wings held out sideways; the smaller, more delicate damselflies settle with their wings along the length of their body.

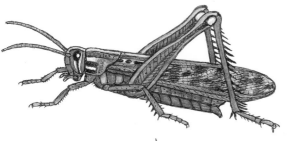

Grasshoppers

Large, often green or brown insects, which "sing" by rubbing their body parts—usually their legs—together to make a high-pitched, repetitive buzzing sound. Usually found in grasslands, where their camouflaged coloration can make them hard to find.

Fireflies

These tiny beetles would be overlooked and little known were it not for one important characteristic: their ability to emit light, which the wingless female produces in order to attract a flying male.

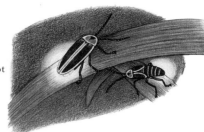

Crickets

Similar to grasshoppers, the courting males also sing, usually by rubbing part of their wing against the other. Also found mainly in grasslands, though one species, the house cricket, has moved into our homes.

Praying mantis

One of our most spectacular insects, this species (also known as the European mantis) is a long, slender green insect that holds its forelegs out in front of it, as if at prayer. Similar to a large grasshopper, it is found in woods, fields, and backyards, mainly in the eastern United States.

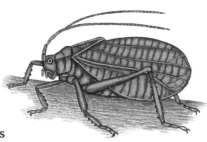

Katydids

From the group known as long-horned grasshoppers, katydids are mainly found in the eastern United States, where they often keep us awake at night with their repetitive song: "katy-did, katy-didn't, katy-did," etc.

Cicadas

Superficially similar to grasshoppers and crickets, though they are not in fact related, being closer to more primitive insects such as leafhoppers and spittlebugs. The name comes from a Latin term meaning "buzzer," due to the repetitive sound the insect makes, generally during the day when the weather is hot.

Ladybugs

These smart little insects are some of the most useful to us of all: farmers and gardeners encourage them because of their habit of eating pests. There are more than 450 different kinds in North America, many of them red with black spots; others may be orange, yellow, or black.

Ants

Among the world's most advanced and successful social insects, living in vast, highly organized colonies with one or more queens at the center, surrounded by willing workers. One of the most familiar is the black carpenter ant, found throughout the eastern United States.

Make a home for minibeasts

When I was growing up we called them "creepy-crawlies" or "bugs." Nowadays we often use the term "minibeasts" to cover the thousands of insects and other invertebrates that we come across in our daily lives. These include true insects—such as flies, bees, wasps, butterflies, and moths (and their caterpillars) and various beetles and bugs—as well as other unrelated groups, such as spiders, snails, and slugs.

The best way to get to know minibeasts is to keep them yourself. By watching them grow and develop, and seeing how they change at different times in their life cycle, you will really begin to appreciate these tiny creatures.

What you need

- A tank: made from glass or plastic, roughly twelve to thirty inches long, twelve to twenty inches wide, and twelve to twenty inches deep—with a secure, tight-fitting lid. You can buy tanks from your local pet store or by mail order from Internet suppliers.
- The filling: the best kind is peat soil—never use compost, as this contains chemicals that will be harmful to the minibeasts.
- Extras: old leaves and rotted wood; dry twigs and small branches; old flowerpots.
- Water: a small plastic dish or old jam jar lid; an atomizer such as the kind your mom uses to spray her houseplants.
- Food: bits of fruit and vegetables.

What to do

Fill the bottom of your tank with soil, to a depth of about four or five inches, and spray it with water to make it damp. Then arrange the twigs, branches, and leaves around inside the tank so the minibeasts have got plenty of places where they can hide or sit. You can also use bits of bark, stones, or old flowerpots to make hiding places. Sink the jam jar lid or plastic dish into the soil and fill with water, then spray again to create a nice, humid atmosphere.

It's now time to introduce your minibeasts. Avoid putting in carnivorous creatures (such as spiders, ladybugs, and centipedes), as they will eat all the others. The best creatures to keep are slugs, snails, woodlice, beetles, and millipedes; they should be able to live happily alongside one another.

You'll also need to provide food: bits of fruit and vegetables are ideal—cut them up into small chunks to make it easier for the minibeasts to carry.

Tips

- ◉ Keep your tank somewhere warm, but not too hot, since it may dry out.
- ◉ Make sure you give your minibeasts a sense of the daily cycle by switching off lights at night.
- ◉ Remove any uneaten food before it turns moldy.
- ◉ After handling minibeasts or the filling in the tank, always wash your hands.
- ◉ If you go on vacation, get someone else to feed your minibeasts and keep the tank clean.

At least two out of every three species on the planet are minibeasts—of which almost 100,000 different kinds live in the United States and Canada. And these are only the ones we know about—there are plenty more out there just waiting to be discovered!

124

Lie down in long grass and stare at the sky

I long for scenes where man has never trod,
A place where woman never smiled or wept;
There to abide with my Creator, God,
And sleep as I in childhood sweetly slept:
Untroubling and untroubled where I lie,
The grass below—above, the vaulted sky.
—JOHN CLARE, FROM "I AM"

For many of us, one of our first childhood memories is the sensation of lying down in long grass and staring up at a clear blue sky; time seemed to stand still.

So why not do it again? It really is a wonderful way to relax and shed the cares of this world.

Become a bat detective

There are about fifty different kinds of bats in the United States and Canada—just over one in ten of all our mammal species—yet apart from the occasional glimpse at dusk on a warm summer's evening, we hardly ever see them. That's because they spend the daylight hours roosting in the attics of houses, old barns or caves, and also in crevices, tree cavities, and thick vegetation, and emerge only at night to hunt for their insect prey.

Some people are put off by all the folklore about bats, so let's get a few things straight. Apart from South American vampire bats, they don't suck blood; they don't get tangled in your hair; and bats are most certainly not blind. In fact, they have pretty good eyesight, although they track down their prey using a very different technique.

Bats hunt by "echolocation"—uttering a series of rapid clicks that "bounce off" any objects in the air. By listening to the echo made when the sound hits the object, the bat knows how close it is, even if it can't actually see it.

Bats also know whether what they are hearing is made by a solid object like a wall, or a moving prey, like a moth—enabling them either to avoid a collision or to catch their supper.

If you want to learn more about bats, the best way is to go on an organized bat walk. These usually take place at dusk during the spring and summer, and are run by local or state bat conservation groups.

Because bats call at very high frequencies—generally too high for the human ear to detect—the group leader will usually bring a "bat detector." This clever instrument can convert the calls into a series of clicks that we are then able to hear.

Different kinds of bats call at different sound frequencies; some bats have very rhythmic calls, and others warble, almost like a bird. So an experienced "bat-man" or "bat-woman" will be able to identify the particular species you are hearing.

On some bat walks, especially later in the year, the leader may look inside bat boxes and bring one out for you to look at. You'll be amazed at how tiny bats are, with such delicate wings—yet the bat is a really impressive flyer, rivaling even the birds with its aerobatic skills.

The smallest North American bat, the western pipistrelle, is less than three inches long (including its tail), with a wingspan of about eight inches. It weighs around one-sixth of an ounce—less than a nickel. The largest, the western bonneted bat, is about four and a half inches long and weighs almost three ounces—about the same as a starling.

Collect birds' feathers

Quite rightly, collecting birds' eggs is against the law. But it's fine to make a collection of feathers—and a great way to learn just what complex structures they are.

For its weight, a feather is one of the strongest objects in the natural world: feathers are capable of carrying birds on journeys of many thousands of miles.

Feathers are made from a substance known as keratin—the same as that found in human hair and nails. It is strong and in-credibly light, as well as flexible enough to withstand the stresses and strains of a bird's aerial existence.

Their structure is a miracle of evolution: a hollow shaft down the center supports hundreds of delicate filaments, known as "barbs," along each side. These mesh together using even tinier filaments known as "barbules," creating a tight and highly effec-tive tool for flight.

Most of the feathers you will find are the larger wing feath-ers, known as "primaries." Because these get so much wear and tear, birds shed them regularly (usually once a year) in a process known as molt. The easiest ones to find are from larger birds such as crows (all black), pigeons (different shades of gray), and gulls (usually gray with black and white on the tip). Park ponds and riverbanks are good places to look for feathers from ducks, geese, and swans.

To examine a feather's structure, run your finger along one of the barbs and see how they come apart, then fit back together—just like the two sides of a zipper. You can also use a magnifying glass to see the individual barbs and barbules. Once you've had a good look, use a pair of scissors to cut open the shaft—revealing its hollow, air-filled interior.

Different birds have a very different number of feathers—smaller birds, such as sparrows and thrushes, have fewer than 5,000; while larger birds, such as the whistling swan, may have more than 25,000 feathers, most of which are on its head and neck. The North American bird with the least number of feathers is the ruby-throated hummingbird, with just 940.

Make an old-fashioned quill pen

You can use larger feathers, like those from a goose or swan, to make an old-fashioned quill pen.

- With an adult's supervision, start by dipping the tip of the feather in boiling water to soften it.
- Again, with an adult's supervision, use a sharp penknife to make a neat, horizontal cut across the end of the feather; then make two diagonal cuts to create a triangular-shaped nib.
- Finally, make a neat cut just under half an inch in length from the tip of the nib back up the handle, and a cut across the tip of the nib.
- Carefully dip your quill into a bottle of ink, allowing the ink to rise up the shaft of the quill.
- Then start to write. This will take practice at first; quill pens are rather messy—but with a bit of effort you'll soon master the art.

Spend the night in a tent in your backyard

Even the most familiar place can seem strange and mysterious when experienced at night—and nowhere more so than your own backyard. So choose a fine, warm summer night, pitch your tent with plenty of time to spare, and get everything you need for a night's adventure.

- Sleeping bags to keep you warm.
- Blow-up mattresses or something soft to lie on.
- A flashlight, plus a spare.
- Food and drink for a midnight snack.

One of the nicest things about sleeping out in your yard is that in spring or summer you'll be woken up by the sound of the dawn chorus. Open the flaps of your tent and just enjoy from the comfort of your bed the sensation of hearing this wonderful orchestra of birdsong.

Make a compost heap

My mother was an avid gardener, and like anyone brought up during World War II had a fanatical loathing of waste. So any grass cuttings, vegetable peelings, or dead leaves would be taken in a wheelbarrow down to the end of the yard, and flung onto the compost heap. Little did I realize then that this smelly pile of rotting vegetation might be home to reptiles such as snakes and lizards. If I had, I might have dared to take a closer look.

Wildlife just love compost heaps—which are the equivalent of a centrally heated home with a diner attached. It's not just reptiles that are attracted by the warmth generated by all that decomposing compost: slugs, snails, and other minibeasts all make their home there, sometimes attracting birds to feed on them.

And compost heaps are a more environmentally friendly way of providing compost—much better to use recycled leftovers than to buy peat-based composts, whose production causes harm to the environment. Every home should have one.

What kind of compost heap should I have?

You have three basic choices:

- The loose heap: simply a pile in your yard—easy for animals to get in and out of but not so efficient at generating heat.
- The boxed heap: easily constructed with bits of wood and chicken wire—more efficient though less accessible.
- The fancy composter: these can be bought from garden centers or by mail order, and have a range of different chambers so that you can get easy access to compost at different stages of the decomposition process.

Where to put your compost heap

A hidden corner of your yard is best, since it will be out of the way—but avoid too shady a spot; compost needs some sunshine to stop it from getting waterlogged. The area should also be reasonably level so that your heap will be stable.

What you need to make a boxed heap

- Four wooden fence posts—roughly four by four inches across and approximately four to five feet long.
- Wooden planks or chicken wire to make the sides.
- Straw or small twigs for drainage.
- A heavy-duty mallet.
- Nails or tacks.
- A layer of carpet, tarpaulin, or heavy-duty plastic sheeting.

How to make the heap

⊙ Start by hammering the four fence posts firmly into the ground.
⊙ Next, either nail the planks to the posts, or tack the chicken wire around them—but make sure one side is easy to open, allowing you to remove the compost when it's ready to use.
⊙ Line the bottom of the box with the straw or twigs.
⊙ Then start the process by adding your garden waste in layers about six to eight inches thick, alternating grass cuttings, leaves, and so on with a thin layer of soil in between.
⊙ Add water if the material is too dry.
⊙ Finally, when the layers have reached the top, cover with the piece of carpet, tarpaulin, or plastic sheeting, and secure the lid.
⊙ Wait about three months while the compost "cooks," then open your front hatch to remove it for use.

THINGS YOU CAN PUT IN	THINGS TO AVOID
fallen leaves	backyard chemicals
vegetable and fruit peelings	dog or cat waste
shredded paper	any meat product
used tea bags	thick woody stems or twigs
weeds	anything man-made
hedge clippings	leftover food
grass cuttings	anything that might grow— seed heads, roots, etc.
dead leaves	

The ideal internal temperature of your compost heap should range from 120 to 150 degrees Fahrenheit, though temperatures can rise as high as 160 degrees—warm enough to heat up a mug of tea or cook an egg!

Go on a city safari

Cities are often known as "urban jungles"—and you might think that this would mean wild creatures would struggle to find a home there. But far from being tough, hostile environments for wildlife, they in fact provide everything the creature-about-town needs.

Whether a wild animal is looking for food, water, shelter, light, or heat, the modern city provides it. As a result, a whole host of animals—and of course plants—have moved downtown.

They're not just surviving there, but thriving. Every single major animal group—from birds of prey to deer and from seabirds to seals—can be found in at least one North American city. And because these animals have gotten used to living alongside millions of us, they are often far less wary than their country cousins.

Take the urban coyote. In the countryside, coyotes are shy creatures, rarely seen apart from a bushy tail disappearing rapidly out of sight. Yet in our towns and cities they will stroll down the street without a care in the world.

One of the best ways to get to know the wildlife of a town or city is to treat it just like any other place to watch wildlife—and go on an urban safari. By planning your route so it takes in a range of different locations and habitats, you should see not only a wide variety of plants and animals but enjoy great views as well.

Tips

- ⚙ Get hold of a detailed city map, ideally one that shows the areas between the built-up areas as well as the street plan.
- ⚙ Plan your route—try to include a patch of trees, the city park, a river or (if you are on the coast) the shoreline—each new habitat is likely to bring new sightings.
- ⚙ Take a pair of binoculars, a couple of field guides, and a notebook to write down what you see.
- ⚙ As always, a digital camera is a good way to record sightings (especially of plants and insects) for you to identify later, when you get home.
- ⚙ Don't forget to look down—cities, and especially ports like New York and San Francisco, have all sorts of exotic foreign plants growing in some unlikely places.

Classic city locations and what to look for

- **Atlanta, Georgia:** As one of the most heavily wooded of all U.S. cities, Atlanta is great for forest birds such as woodpeckers, thrushes and tanagers, wild turkeys, and deer. Check out the city parks, Chattahoochee River, and the woodlands around the Fernbank Science Center about six miles from the city's heart.

- **Boston, Massachusetts:** Its position on the Atlantic seaboard makes Boston a real hot spot for shorebirds; Wilson's storm-petrel is a regular visitor to the harbor! Raccoons, coyotes, and opossums are common, though not always easy to see—check out the Boston Nature Center, which has two miles of trails and boardwalks through a range of habitats.

- **Chicago, Illinois:** Its location on the south shore of Lake Erie makes Chicago a magnet for migrating birds in spring and autumn, especially in bad weather, when millions of warblers, vireos, thrushes, and other songbirds may be grounded and seek shelter in the city parks. White-tailed deer, cottontail rabbits, and gray squirrels are also a familiar sight.

- **Los Angeles, California:** Being on the Pacific seaboard makes L.A. a hot spot for marine life, including seals and sea lions. Its southwesterly location brings in a range of Californian specialties such as monarch butterflies and the California ground squirrel. Oh, and Beverly Hills hosts coyotes as well as the rich and famous!

- **Miami, Florida:** The Hispanic influence in this southeastern metropolis goes far beyond the human beings. Miami is also home to several introduced parrot species, brought here from Central and South America and released by accident. During the winter in particular its warm climate makes it the ideal habitat for northern birds seeking food and shelter—check out Enchanted Forest Elaine Gordon Park and Arch Creek Park to the north of the city.

- **New York City:** Two of the best places to get close-up views of birds in the whole of the United States are in New York City—Jamaica Bay, on the outskirts, and Central Park, in the heart of Manhattan. On good days in spring or fall you can see over twenty different kinds of warblers in Central Park, while the shores of Jamaica Bay are home to resident and migrant shorebirds, ducks, and other waterfowl. All the usual urban mammals live here, too, with raccoons raiding trash cans a not uncommon occurrence. And, of course, Central Park is also home to the most famous pair of red-tailed hawks in America, Pale Male and Lola!

- **Orlando, Florida:** Visit Disney World for a great range of herons, egrets, and other waterbirds that are so tame you might think they must be in a zoo! Deer, bobcats, armadillos, and alligators are also a regular sight.

- **San Francisco, California:** The Bay Area (and cities such as Monterey and Pacific Grove a couple of hours to the south) are a paradise for wildlife: from sea otters to shorebirds and monarch butterflies to acorn woodpeckers. If you have time, go on a whale watch off Monterey to get close encounters with whales, dolphins, and oceangoing seabirds, such as petrels, shearwaters, and albatrosses.

- **Seattle, Washington:** Puget Sound on the Pacific coastline near Seattle is one of the best places for wildlife watching in North America, with whales, waterfowl, and other marine life. Explore the city itself for a wide range of birds, including bald eagles, our national bird.

- **Washington, D.C.:** The combination of two rivers and so much greenery provided by the city parks, together with its southerly location, make Washington a great place for a city safari. Look out for turkey vultures and ospreys, flights of American nighthawks at dusk, and mammals such as raccoons after dark.

Austin, the state capital of Texas, is home to one of the most amazing wildlife spectacles in the whole of North America—perhaps on the planet. Every evening in the spring and summer months up to one million Mexican free-tailed bats emerge at dusk from beneath the Congress Avenue Bridge, swarming like flies before they go off to feed for the night.

How to identify . . .
amphibians

Not only are North America's frogs, toads, newts, and salamanders a fascinating group of creatures, but they also serve as vital indicators of the health of our natural environment—especially during a time of rapid environmental change. More than any other animals their specialized lifestyles—spending much of the time on land but requiring water in order to breed and raise their young—means they are adversely affected by any changes to the environment.

As many ponds, lakes, and marshes are drained for development, amphibians are under threat as never before. Disease is another problem, as is water pollution. And finally climate change threatens the populations of several species. So if you do come across any amphibians, make sure you don't disturb them, as they need all the help they can get.

How to identify . . .
amphibians

Green tree frog

Medium-size tree frog, and as its name suggests, usually green in color, though like other frogs very variable. Creamy stripe along its sides also distinctive. Found in the southeastern United States, in swamps and other damp places.

American bullfrog

North America's largest frog, up to six inches long (though the record stands at a whopping eight inches). Plain green above (though in the Southeast, especially Florida, it is often darker and more mottled) and pale below. Usually found near the edges of ponds and marshes, or among floating plants, where males utter their extraordinary calls. Predatory and voracious, it eats almost anything it can swallow.

Arizona tree frog

Also known as the canyon tree frog, this species is found in the southwestern United States, especially Arizona and New Mexico. Medium-size and gray-brown in color, it is mainly a nocturnal hunter. Well adapted to desert life, though like all frogs it requires water in which to lay its eggs.

Little grass frog

The smallest North American frog, barely half an inch long, and as a result usually mistaken for a young of another frog species. Varies in color from pale pink through green to brown, but always shows a thick, dark stripe through the eye and along its sides. Confined to southeastern states, especially Florida.

American toad

The most widespread toad of the northeastern states, usually plain brown in color, but some individuals (especially females) may show brighter patterning. Less tied to water than frogs, toads are often found in damp areas in our backyards, so long as there are plenty of insects on which they can feed.

Wood frog

A smallish, plain frog with a distinctive dark mask giving it a "robberlike" appearance. Widespread across the northern part of the continent (farther north than any other American amphibian or reptile), and may call when ice is still on the surface of ponds.

Eastern (red-spotted) newt

Common and widespread in the eastern United States, this newt has a highly complex life cycle, with the young (known as red efts) living on land, even though the adults are aquatic. Very variable in appearance, but red spots always present.

Plains spadefoot

Closely related to true toads, spadefoots have, as their name suggests, sharp spurs on their hind feet to enable them to dig down into sandy soil to stay moist and avoid being eaten. Be careful handling them: they often provoke allergic reactions. The plains spadefoot is mainly found on the Great Plains.

Mud puppy (water dog)

This species of giant salamander can grow to over a foot long (the record is over nineteen inches), yet it retains its larval characteristics—including feathery gills—for its whole life. In northern states it's known as the water dog, due to its aquatic and carnivorous habits.

Eastern tiger salamander

One of our most striking amphibians, with a combination of yellowish and black blotches that give the creature its name. Found in the eastern United States, usually in deep water, where it breeds early in the year.

Northern leopard frog

Once so common it was used in high school biology classes, this species has undergone a major decline, though it is still found right across the northern United States. Green, with distinctive round, dark spots on its back.

Barred tiger salamander

Found mainly in the central states of the United States, the barred tiger has a bolder pattern than the other salamanders, with large black and yellow blotches. Often used as fish bait, however, so it may turn up outside its normal range.

Spotted salamander

A mainly dark salamander with a variable number of distinctive yellow-orange spots. Usually appears in early spring, after the first warm rains that stimulate it to begin breeding. Found throughout the northeastern United States and down as far as Texas.

Look for snakes and lizards

In the days of the Wild West and beyond, it used to be said that the only good snake was a dead one. In a country with many venomous snakes, including cottonmouths, copperheads, and the huge and notorious rattlesnakes, this perhaps wasn't so surprising, but fortunately most people now take a more enlightened attitude toward these fascinating and often beautiful creatures.

But you should still take great care, especially in areas where venomous snakes are known to live. To keep you and those around you safe there are some obvious things to remember:

- If you come across a snake, NEVER scream or shout, make a loud noise (for example, calling out to someone), or make sudden movements. If you panic, and frighten the snake, you increase your chances of being attacked and/or bitten. By the way, although snakes don't have ears, they do feel the vibrations produced by a human voice.
- Stay at a safe distance—at least one body length of the snake away and preferably more. If you are already closer than that when you notice the snake, move slowly, quietly, and carefully back until you are out of range.
- Never try to catch or kill a snake—almost all the people who are bitten by a snake are trying to catch or kill it.
- If you want the snake to be removed (for example, from your backyard) call a professional, who will do it without harming themselves, you, or the snake.
- Remember—snakes don't attack people unless they have a very good reason to do so—so treat a snake with respect and it will leave you alone!

In the very unlikely event that you (or someone you are with) are bitten by a snake, here's what to do:

- Seek immediate medical care—call your local doctor or dial 911.

- Stay calm—becoming agitated will allow the venom to circulate more quickly in your bloodstream.
- Suck or squeeze as much venom as you can out of the wound—or get someone else to do so. Venom will NOT harm you when taken orally.
- If you have been bitten on a finger or arm remove any jewelry, as the organ may swell up.
- Keep the area bitten below the heart—as low as possible. But DON'T use a tourniquet, since this can cause more harm than good. And DON'T use ice—this also makes things worse.
- If you can identify the snake WITHOUT anyone coming to further harm, try to do so—it will help the medics decide on the best treatment for you.

All this sounds quite scary, but remember that very few people are accidentally bitten by snakes, and the vast majority make a full recovery. And also remember that the vast majority of snakes you will come across are NOT venomous (venomous snakes constitute only about 5 percent of U.S. snake species)—though to avoid being bitten you should still follow the advice above.

So if I haven't scared you out of your wits, how do you see a snake or lizard?!

- Go to the right location: snakes and lizards are quite fussy about where they live. Some, like water snakes and most garter snakes, are found in marshes, rivers, and streams; others, like corn snakes and fence lizards, prefer drier areas such as rocky hillsides or deserts.
- Go at the right time of year: because snakes and lizards are cold-blooded, they can't regulate their temperature themselves as we and other mammals can; those living in northern areas hibernate during the autumn and winter. The best times to see these species are on warm, sunny days in spring or autumn when they have either just come out of hibernation, or are about to go back in.

- Go during the right weather: warm, sunny days are ideal, because snakes and lizards emerge to soak up the sun's rays and warm their bodies. But you can also try looking just after a shower or longer spell of rain: as the sun comes out, so do the reptiles.

- Go at the right time of day: as the sun rises in the sky and heats up the ground, snakes and lizards begin to emerge from their hiding places. This is often the best time of day to find them, when they bask in the sun to warm up. Later on, as the sun's heat increases, they are harder to find and no longer need to stay out in the open to keep warm. Late afternoon to early evening is also a good time; reptiles often sunbathe once the temperature begins to drop.

- Look in the right place: seek out sunny areas on south-facing slopes, sheltered from the wind. Snakes and lizards will use these as sun traps, lying flat against the ground in order to make the most of the sun's warmth.

- Look in the right way: walk slowly and steadily. Reptiles are very sensitive to movement and will slink away if you approach too quickly. Keep the sun behind you, but watch your shadow; this, too, will disturb a basking reptile.

- Look for signs: snakes and lizards have to shed their skin from time to time, to enable them to grow, so you may find dis-carded skins—a sure sign that reptiles are in the area.

- Listen: when a snake or lizard moves it rustles the vegetation— so if you hear something move, wait quietly for a few minutes to see if it comes out.

Rattlesnakes hunt by night using heat-seeking "pits" just below their nostrils that enable them to detect the tiny amount of warmth given out by rodents or small birds. So when a mouse, for instance, walks past the snake it can work out exactly where to strike—without seeing its prey at all!

Pick (and eat) blackberries

During World War II fresh fruit was hard to get, so blackberries were a welcome addition to the meager wartime diet. My grandmother told me that one day a neighbor stopped by with some blackberries, and started to hand them out to the children without washing them first. My grandmother was horrified. "Won't they have maggots in them?" she asked. "Maybe," replied her neighbor as the children stuffed their faces with the juicy fruit. "But the way I sees it, them that eats most blackberries, gets most maggots!"

Blackberries are the best free food in the countryside—easy to find, easy to pick (as long as you're careful of the prickles on the bramble bushes), and great to eat.

The first ripe blackberries appear during June or July, depending on where you live. Unripe blackberries are small, hard, and either green or red—so wait until you can see big bunches of black ones before you go on a picking expedition.

Take a container to put them in, and a pair of thin but strong gardening gloves to avoid your hands being pricked or getting stained—though some people don't mind getting a bit messy.

And try not to eat too many while you're picking them—it'll take you twice as long to collect enough to make something delicious once you get them home.

Some easy blackberry recipes

Blackberry and Apple Crumble

- Mix 1 cup plain flour and 1 stick cold butter (chopped up into cubes) in a bowl until they are crumbled; then mix in ½ cup of sugar.
- Wash 2 pounds of apples, remove the cores, and peel and slice them, then arrange in the bottom of a large shallow dish rubbed with a little butter.
- Wash a couple of handfuls of blackberries, pat them dry, and then put them on top of the apple slices.
- Sprinkle ½ cup demerara or light brown sugar over the fruit.
- Spread the crumble mixture evenly on top.
- Bake at 350°F for 40 to 50 minutes, until the topping gets nice and brown.
- Tastes great with cream, ice cream, or custard.

Blackberry Fool

- Purée about 2 cups of blackberries with ⅓ to ½ cup sugar in a blender, then push through a sieve to remove the pips.
- Add the juice of a lemon (to taste).
- Whisk ¾ cup heavy cream until it starts to thicken.
- Fold the cream into the blackberry purée.
- Garnish with a few fresh blackberries and serve.

Blackberry Jelly

This is a really good one, since it's one of the few jellies that doesn't need extra pectin in order to set—the blackberries themselves contain enough.

- Wash a pound or so of cooking apples and cut them into quarters. You don't need to peel or core them.
- Put the apples into a saucepan with 4 cups water and the juice of a lemon, and stew them gently over a low heat until they go soft.
- While the apples are cooking, wash 4 pounds (about 12 cups) of blackberries and pat them dry.
- Add the blackberries to the apples and cook them until the mixture goes soft.
- Turn the mixture into a muslin bag suspended over a second clean pan, and leave overnight.
- The next day, add 1½ cups of sugar for every 2 cups of juice, giving the mixture a good stir until the sugar has dissolved completely.
- Sterilize some jars by washing them thoroughly and drying them in the oven at 200°F for about half an hour.
- Bring the juice and sugar mixture to a boil and simmer gently, stirring from time to time, for 10 to 15 minutes.

Test whether the jelly is set by dipping a very cold teaspoon into the mixture. If a few seconds after you take the spoon out of the pan it starts to thicken and stick to the spoon, the jelly is ready.

Pour the mixture into the warm jars, cover them, and let them cool.

How to identify . . .

roadside flowers
and plants

As we drive past, it's easy to ignore the common roadside flowers and plants that line our roads and freeways. Yet if you stop
to take a closer look you will see a wonderful range of blooms,
whose yellows, blues, and purples bring a welcome splash of
color to our lives.

   With literally thousands of different species to choose from,
you may struggle to identify everything you find. But most of
us can recognize the common families—poppies, daisies, etc.—
and others, like sunflowers, are familiar backyard plants. But
you don't need to know the name of every plant—just enjoy the
beauty they bring to our lives.

How to identify . . .
roadside flowers and plants

Forget-me-not
A group of more than a hundred different species, mostly tall, with small and delicate white flowers with yellow centers; though sometimes flowers may be yellow, and cultivated ones found in backyards are usually blue.

California poppy
This tall, colorful poppy is one of the classic flowers of the western United States, growing on grasslands, meadows, and roadsides all over the region. Up to two feet tall, with a shade ranging from deep orange through yellow, and in bloom from February through September.

Dandelion
One of our commonest, most widespread, and most successful wildflowers, though often dismissed as a "weed"! Incredibly good at colonizing new areas, using its light seeds, each with its own parachute. Combination of fluffy yellow flowers and tooth-shaped leaves are unmistakable.

Wild rose
This charming relative of all the world's cultivated roses is a simple yet elegant plant, with five simple petals— usually pale pink in color. As with all roses, beware of the sharp thorns, and look for for the fruits (or "hips") in late summer.

Common buttercup
Also known as the tall buttercup, this alien invader (from Europe) is commonly seen on roadsides and in meadows throughout the United States, from May through September. Tall, with bright, buttery yellow, flowers.

Meadowsweet

A member of the rose family, with pale pink or white flowers arranged in a tight, bushy cluster. Mainly found in the eastern United States, along roadsides, from July through September.

Sunflower

One of our largest and most distinctive plants, with the huge, golden-yellow flowers that give the species its name. Common along roadsides and in fields and prairies, from June through October.

Oxeye daisy

Our commonest and most widespread daisy, a familiar sight along roadsides, and in fields and meadows, throughout the United States, from May through October. Very tall (up to thirty inches), with classic daisy flowers—white with yellow centers.

Goldenrod

A member of the daisy family, its attractive, tall, golden-yellow flowers are characterized by their fluffy flower heads and long, slender leaves. Found throughout the United States, in bloom from June through November.

Queen Anne's lace

A tall plant—up to five feet—with distinctive flat clusters of tiny, creamy white flowers, and a single, darker flower in the center, which the plant uses to attract flies and other insects for pollination. Found throughout the United States and in bloom from May through October.

Yucca plant

This tall plant is characteristic of dry areas of the United States, especially in the West. The long center stem carries a cluster of pale, pinkish white flowers, pollinated by a particular group of moths.

Naughty stuff

Typical of boys of my generation (and quite a few girls, too), I loved making weapons out of anything I could find outdoors. Sometimes this simply involved picking the end off a plant and using it as a dart or pellet; other forms of attack were more complex and time-consuming—and all were great fun! Children are probably now discouraged from doing these things because of spurious health and safety fears—but here they are anyway.

Make itching powder from rose hips

Open up a rose hip, take a close look, and you'll see that the seeds are encased in tiny hairs. When put down the back of a classmate's shirt, they cause an unpleasant itching—a trick used by generations of high school kids to liven up a dull lesson.

Use seeds and grasses as darts and pellets

In late summer, all kinds of grasses produce seeds or seed heads that can be used as pellets or darts.

Some of my favorites are

- ❂ Wild barley: pull off the end to use as a highly effective dart— not only is it a straight and accurate flyer, but it also sticks to wool and fleece.
- ❂ Plantain: the stems of the introduced English plantain (also

known as ribwort plantain) can be wound around one another to flick off the heads—creating a very satisfying pellet, which can be aimed accurately at your opponent.

- Burdock: the sticky seed heads of this common plant are ideal for throwing at unsuspecting friends, since they stick to almost anything.
- Grass whistle: this is a less antisocial game—simply pick a broad blade of grass, put it between your palms, and blow. With practice you should be able to produce a range of satisfying (and sometimes rude) sounds.
- Cleavers: this annual plant spreads its seeds via a fruit with hooked barbs that attach to any animal passing by—including us. They make a splendid missile, as, like the burdock, they stick to almost anything. Among the folk names for cleavers are beggar's-lice, everlasting friendship, stick-a-back, and, my favorite, sticky-willy.

plantain

cleavers

Burdock is so sticky it inspired the inventor of Velcro—the product used in many modern items of clothing as an alternative to zippers or buttons. Some children now call burdock "the Velcro plant" as a result.

burdock

wild barley

Things to do with wildflowers

Wildflowers are among our most beautiful natural objects, bringing a welcome splash of color to all sorts of places, from roadsides to hedgerows, and forest clearings to city center sidewalks. Our grandparents' generation used them for dozens of things: here are just a few.

Pick a bunch of wildflowers and press them

In Victorian times, every young lady—and many young men— would eagerly await the spring and summer months, when they could pick bunches of wildflowers and present them to their intended as a token of their undying love.

But cut flowers would last only a few days, so one way to keep them longer was to press them. Flower pressing was especially popular among the aristocratic classes, and Queen Victoria herself enjoyed the pastime.

The tradition of drying wildflowers to preserve them goes back much longer than this: examples have been found in ancient Egyptian tombs and Renaissance Bibles.

Although pressed flowers are still often used by artists and craftspeople, most children (and indeed quite a few adults) have never enjoyed this simple pleasure. Why? Mainly because many conservationists keep banging on about how terrible it is to pick wildflowers.

To which I say . . . nonsense! If you are going to learn about nature, you need to get real, hands-on experience. And while digging up wildflowers to replant them in your backyard shouldn't be encouraged, picking a few blooms to take home really isn't going to do any harm. So once you've gathered your favorite flowers, why not press them to keep them looking almost as good as the day they were picked?

What you need

- A sealable plastic box to collect your specimens.
- A large, heavy book (old phone directories are ideal).
- Some plain white paper.
- A heavy weight—either a couple of bricks, or a large plastic container you can fill with water and seal up.
- A flat piece of wood (or a tray)—to be placed between the weight and the book to make sure you press evenly.
- A pair of tweezers to handle the delicate pressed flowers without damaging them.
- Clear glue.
- Scissors.
- Adhesive plastic film to protect the design.
- The flowers themselves: almost any small, simple bloom will do, such as buttercups, poppies, daisies, or forget-me-nots.

Tip

Make sure the flowers are as fresh as possible. Ideally, press them immediately after picking; but if you can't, store them in a plastic bag or box in the fridge. Don't add water, since this will speed up the decaying process.

What to do next

- Arrange your flowers on a sheet of paper, with the flowers separated so they don't touch one another.
- Cover with a second sheet of paper, and put inside your large book, leaving at least half an inch of pages between each set of flowers.

- Place the flat piece of wood or tray on top of the book, and put the weights on top.
- After about a week, remove the weights and open the book carefully.
- Using the tweezers, delicately lift each flower off the paper, taking great care not to damage the petals.

Once you have enough specimens, you can make all sorts of lovely designs by arranging them on white or colored poster board (pastel shades are best), then sticking them down using clear glue.

To protect your finished design, you can cover it with adhesive plastic film, then trim with scissors to the required size and shape.

You can then turn your designs into simple greetings cards or bookmarks, or put them in photo frames as gifts—a lovely memory of a summer's walk in the forest, woods, or meadows.

Make elderflower fritters and elderflower cordial

Depending on where you live, elderflowers (the flowers of the elderberry shrub) bloom between late spring and early summer. Try to pick them when they have just come into bloom, since they will taste fresher—and have fewer insects on them.

And if you can, avoid picking flowers growing right next to a busy road (they may have traces of pollution), or near farm fields, where they may have been sprayed with chemicals.

Don't be put off by the flowers' rather odd smell—they have a wonderful flavor, as these two very different recipes show.

Elderflower Fritters

INGREDIENTS
I egg
⅓ to ½ cup milk
¼ cup plain flour
sunflower oil
5 elderflower heads, unwashed
sugar to dip

METHOD
1. Separate the egg into white and yolk.
2. In a bowl, mix the egg yolk, milk, and flour together until
   smooth; put aside for about 20 minutes.
3. In another bowl, whisk the egg white until it begins to show
   "peaks"; then fold gently into the batter mixture.
4. Heat an inch or so of sunflower oil in a deep-sided pan until
   it is almost smoking.
5. Shake each of the elderflower heads to remove small insects
   but do not wash them (this will remove the flavor). Dip each
   elderflower head by the stem into the batter; then drop into
   the hot oil. Cook for I or 2 minutes, until it starts to turn
   golden brown.
6. Take out of the oil and place head-down on paper towels to
   drain off excess oil.
7. Dip into the sugar and serve while still piping hot.

Elderflower Cordial

INGREDIENTS
20 elderflower heads, unwashed
up to 4 pounds (9 cups) sugar
5 cups water; boiled, then left to cool
zest and juice of 4 oranges
zest and fruit of 2 lemons
3 ounces citric acid (available from your local pharmacist)

METHOD

1. Trim the flower heads, removing as much stalk as possible. Shake to remove insects, then put the flower heads in a very large bowl or saucepan. Do not wash them, as this will remove the flavor.

2. In a separate saucepan, add the sugar and water. Bring to a boil and stir until the sugar has dissolved. Remove from the heat.

3. Pare the zest from the oranges and lemons and add to the bowl with the elderflowers. Juice the oranges and add this to the bowl, along with the lemons cut into slices.

4. Pour over the hot syrup, stirring to mix the flower heads and fruits, and then stir in the citric acid. Cover with a clean cloth and leave at room temperature for 24 hours.

5. The next day, strain the liquid through a sieve lined with muslin and pour it into clean bottles with screw tops, and store in the fridge. This can be used like a cordial, diluted with about 6 to 10 parts water, depending on your taste. It works especially well with sparkling water.

Blow dandelion clocks

All through the summer, as dandelion flowers turn into seeds, you can play a game with them. Break off the stalk carefully, making sure you don't shake it, since the seeds will fall off before you are ready. Then blow the seeds off the stalk, counting each time you do so. If it takes three puffs to blow off all the seeds, it's three o'clock; four puffs, four o'clock; and so on.

This game has a serious purpose—it reminds us that some flowers' seeds, including those of the dandelion, are dispersed by the wind. It also helps very young children learn to count!

Other dandelion games include making bracelets from the stalks and splitting the stalks to blow sounds through them.

The name "dandelion" comes from the French dent de lion, *meaning "lion's tooth," because of the jagged shape of the leaves.*

Make a daisy chain

There is a flower, a little flower,
With silver crest and golden eye . . .
—JAMES MONTGOMERY

The daisy—whose name literally means "day's eye"—is surely our most common and familiar wildflower. As with so many other common or garden-variety things in nature, we often take it for granted.

Nevertheless, this modest little flower can be used in one of the simplest of all pastimes: making a daisy chain.

The process couldn't be simpler: just pick a couple dozen daisies, leaving the stalk as long as you can. Then use your fingernail or a sharp penknife to split each stalk halfway along, and thread the next daisy through the gap. Carry on until you have enough for a bracelet, a necklace, or even a skipping rope.

It's sometimes said that spring hasn't really arrived until you can cover nine daisies with your foot.

Rose petals and potpourri

Every summer, the front yard of the house I grew up in was filled with the scent of roses. Like many children, I couldn't resist crushing up the petals in a jar full of water to make "perfume" for my mom. I'm not sure she appreciated the destruction I wrought on her lovely roses in order to make this rather smelly concoction, but to me it brought a touch of the exotic to our suburban lives.

If you want to make something more practical and long-lasting out of rose petals or other garden flowers, how about a potpourri? It's simple to do and can be used in a number of ways—as an ideal birthday present, for instance.

What to do

⊙ In late summer, just as the flowers mature, pick a selection of petals from different-colored plants (which also gives you a mixture of scents). Timing is important—you must pick them before they turn brown.

- Dry the petals, either by leaving them on a tray or by baking them in the oven at a very low heat.
- Using a large jar with a sealable top, add your ingredients in these layers:
  - Rose petals or those from other backyard flowers.
  - A "fixative" such as dried lavender, oakmoss, or orrisroot (available from herbalists or by mail order).
  - Spices: cinnamon, cloves, and nutmeg are ideal for their distinctive, woody scent.
  - A few drops of essential oil such as lavender (or, if you prefer, perfume) to intensify the scent.
- Seal the jar and wait a couple of weeks, shaking it every day or two to mix up the contents.
- Then either sew it into the lining of cushion covers or pillows, or put in an open dish to allow the scent to fill a room.

You can also make rose-petal sandwiches

- Pick a bunch of rose petals and remove the white part at the base.
- Take a half-pound slab of butter, wrap it first in the rose petals, then in aluminum foil or plastic wrap, and leave overnight in a cool place.
- The next morning, spread the "rose butter" onto two thin slices of white bread, add a layer of rose petals to one slice, and sprinkle with a little sugar.
- Top with the other slice of bread and cut in half.
- Eat. Enjoy!

Put a buttercup under your chin to see if you like butter

This is another classic childhood custom that is in danger of dying out, which would be a pity. If you can find a field of buttercups, just pick one flower, and place it under your friend's chin. Then it's your turn. If there's a yellow patch under your chin when you do so, you like butter—and there always is!

This game appears to have originated from the widespread belief that the rich yellow color of butter came because cows ate buttercups—though in fact buttercups are bitter tasting, so cattle and other grazing animals avoid it.

In Ireland, farmers used to rub buttercups onto their cows' udders, which was meant to encourage the cows to produce more milk. This is odd, since it was also said that if you smell a buttercup you will go mad! Both of these are examples of rather misguided folklore.

How to identify . . .

creatures in a rock pool

There are few more enjoyable ways to pass the time than to explore the world of the rock pool—those little oases of water left behind when the tide goes down. At first it may seem as if there is little going on, but take a closer look and you'll notice limpets, whelks, cockles, and mussels clustering on the rocks, and shrimps and tiny fish in the water itself.

Look even closer, perhaps using a face mask to look beneath the surface, and a world of wonder reveals itself—with sea anemones looking for all the world like their floral counterparts as their tentacles wave in the water.

Then take a stroll along the tide line, too—home to razor clams and mermaid's purses, and the odd jellyfish stranded by the tide.

How to identify . . .
creatures in
a rock pool

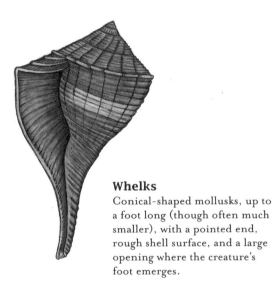

Whelks

Conical-shaped mollusks, up to a foot long (though often much smaller), with a pointed end, rough shell surface, and a large opening where the creature's foot emerges.

Cockles

These heart-shaped marine mollusks are one of our commonest, with several species, including the giant Atlantic cockle, which grows up to five inches across. Look for a pale brown, heart-shaped mollusk with grooves across the shell.

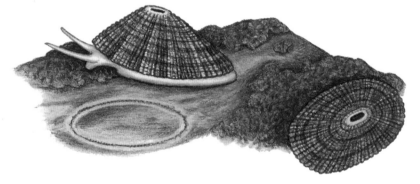

Limpets

Limpets are well known for their ability to stay put however hard you try to dislodge them as they cling to rocks with their suckerlike foot. Yet when the tide comes in, they release their grip and wander around the surface of the rocks, looking for food. Some species then return to exactly the same place.

Mussels

Usually found in huge clusters clinging to the rocks, mussels are a long, pear-shaped shellfish, brown or blackish blue in color, and often covered with tiny barnacles. Mussels feed by filtering tiny marine organisms from the water.

Razor clams

Long, narrow, brownish shell-fish, with rounded ends to the shell, found mainly along the Atlantic and northern Pacific coasts of the United States. Razor clams bury themselves in the sand or mud.

Sea anemones

They may look like plants, but sea anemones—named after the terrestrial flower—are in fact animals that are closely related to corals and jellyfish. At low tide they are easy to miss, looking like lumps of jelly, but when covered with water their tentacles spread out to catch their prey.

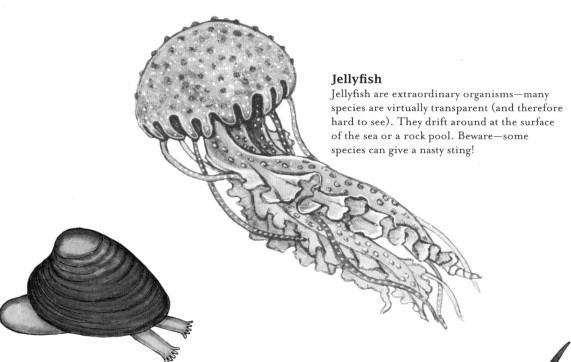

Jellyfish

Jellyfish are extraordinary organisms—many species are virtually transparent (and therefore hard to see). They drift around at the surface of the sea or a rock pool. Beware—some species can give a nasty sting!

Northern quahog

This oval-shaped clam, also known as the cherrystone, with grayish white outer shell and white inner shell, is a common resident of bays and shores along the East Coast of the United States. It has many other names (not least because it is a popular food!), including hard clam, littleneck, topneck, and chowder clam.

Mermaid's purse

Not actually a living creature at all, but the empty egg cases of sharks, rays, and skates, which often wash up on the tide line after the eggs have hatched and young left. Usually oblong, with points at each corner, they look rather like a lady's purse.

Beside the sea

Who can forget summer vacations by the sea, when we paddled along the shore, explored the wonders of rock pools, felt the warm sand between our toes, and enjoyed endless sunshine and freedom? Want to do it all again? Here's how!

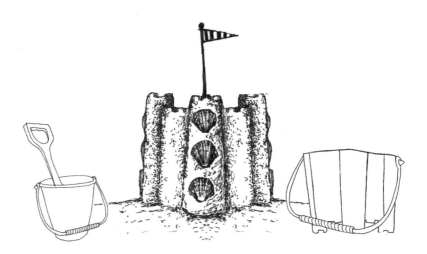

Build a sand castle

This is your chance to become king or queen for a day—making your very own castle out of sand. There really are no limits to what you can achieve—from a simple bucket-shaped tower with a flag stuck on top to a whole complex of fortifications, turrets, moats, and drawbridges.

What you need

- Buckets and pails—ideally a set ranging in size from large to small.
- Shovels—basic plastic ones will do, but wooden ones with a metal blade give a cleaner cut and won't break.
- Plastic knives to smooth the surface of your sandcastle.
- Stuff to decorate the finished structure--flags, shells, pebbles, bits of driftwood, plastic toys . . .
- And, of course, sand—fairly wet sand works best, as you can mold it into shapes easily without it collapsing or crumbling.

The best time to make a sand castle is just as the tide is going out, when the sand a few feet above the tide line is still quite wet.

How to build it

- Start by drawing a circle in the sand—from about one yard to three or four yards across.
- Then excavate the moat for your castle, digging down into the sand around the edge of your circle, to a depth of between eight and twelve inches or so.
- As you dig, pile up the sand to make a wall around the inside of your moat—this will be the main wall of the castle complex.
- To make the turrets, fill your bucket up with sand, making sure it's packed in tightly at the bottom, then pat down the sand at the top of the bucket to make a smooth, flat surface.
- Turn your bucket upside down and give it a sharp bang on the top with your shovel. Then carefully lift the bucket up, wiggling it if the sand won't come out.
- If you've got the consistency of the sand just right, you'll have a lovely neat sand castle—if you haven't, try again with slightly drier or wetter sand until you find the right consistency.
- Smooth any rough edges with a plastic knife.
- Then decorate your castle with the pebbles, shells, etc.
- You can also use the buckets to fill your moat with seawater.

If you've found the right place between the low and high tide lines, you can wait and watch as the tide comes in and floods your day's work. But don't worry—you can come back and build an even better one tomorrow.

starfish

seaweed

Collect seashells

Lots of vacation resorts along our coasts have stores selling exotic seashells for you to buy, but it's much more fun to make your own collection. All you need is a bucket to carry them in. . . .

Take a walk along any sandy beach—ideally at low tide or when the tide is going out. As you wander along the tide line, look for shells—either washed up on the surface or half buried in the sand. Try putting a large shell (such as a whelk) to your ear to hear the sound of the sea.

Once you've got enough shells in your bucket, take them to a rock pool and give them a good cleaning. If you come across a shell with something living inside it, examine it closely, and then put it back in the rock pool.

Most of the shells you find will be common "bivalves" (creatures whose shell divides into two halves), such as cockles or mussels. You may also find snail-like shells such as the whelk, or razor clams—long, straight shells that look like an old-fashioned razor. If you're very lucky, you may even come across beautiful scallop shells.

"She sells seashells on the seashore" is one of the toughest tongue twisters in the English language. Try saying it five times in a row without stopping.

Go on a seaweed hunt

Despite their rather dull name, the various organisms that we know as "seaweed" are some of the most extraordinary living things on the planet.

Once considered to be lowly members of the plant kingdom, the nine thousand or so different kinds of seaweeds are now classified as algae. They come in all sorts of different shapes and sizes, many of which can be found along any stretch of beach.

Seaweed lives and grows by the process of photosynthesis—so just like plants, it needs food, water, and light. That's why seaweed mainly occurs in shallow water—which is where to look for it. The best beaches for seaweeds are usually rocky ones, where they can find a secure place to fix themselves using their "holdfast."

And the best time to look is during a low or receding tide, when you can scramble across the rocks. Watch out—weed-covered rocks can be very slippery, so wear rubber-soled shoes rather than doing this with bare feet or in flip-flops.

One of the most familiar seaweeds, found between the high and low tide lines on any rocky beach, is known as "bladder wrack." The bladders along the long, brown fronds are filled with air so that when the tide comes in the fronds lift in the water and are better able to reach up toward the light. Try popping them and see what happens.

Seaweeds are used for all sorts of things, including food (the Welsh make a delicacy called laver bread from red seaweed and oats), fertilizers, and medicine, especially in Eastern cultures. Seaweed fiber has even been made into environmentally friendly clothing such as T-shirts. Seaweed is also used to forecast the weather—if you hang it up, and watch whether it turns damp or stays dry, you are supposed to be able to tell if it's going to rain.

Explore rock pools by the seaside

When the tide goes out, many sea creatures risk exposure to the sun and wind, which would quickly dry them out if they stayed put. So they seek refuge (or get trapped as the tide recedes) in rock pools—little oases of cool water where they can be safe until the tide comes back in, and they can feed again.

Thus the few hours when the tide is at its lowest is a great time to explore rock pools—you'll be amazed at what you can find.

blennie   *limpet*

What you need

- Containers such as plastic buckets or containers filled with seawater (clear ones are good, since they allow you to see what you have caught from all angles).
- A small fishing net or two (sold at tackle stores and seaside shops).
- A magnifying glass for close inspection.
- Sturdy rubber-soled shoes or water shoes, as rocks may be both slippery and sharp.
- A sun hat and/or sunscreen.
- Sunglasses—especially those with polarized lenses, which make it much easier to see beneath the surface of the water on a sunny day.
- A field guide to coastal creatures.

You can also make yourself an underwater periscope, using a large plastic bottle (the larger the better!). Use scissors or a sharp knife to cut the bottom off. Then put it most of the way into the water, with the top of the bottle above the surface—and simply look through it.

Tips

- Check the tide tables to make sure you've got your timing right—remember the highest and lowest tides coincide with the full and new moon each month, and are also around the time of the spring and autumn equinoxes.
- Always be aware of a rising tide so you don't get cut off as the waters return. If in doubt, seek local advice.
- Take your time—at first sight a rock pool may look empty, but if you watch and wait you'll soon see signs of life.
- Be gentle handling what you find—these are living creatures with soft bodies that can be easily damaged if you're rough with them.
- Lift stones or rocks carefully—there may be creatures hiding beneath them.
- Once you've had a good look, put things back where you found them.
- And be careful—both limpets and barnacles can be sharp!

What to look for

- Fish: small fish often get stranded at low tide and have to wait until the tide comes in to get back out to sea. Other kinds of fish make a permanent home in rock pools. Use your net to catch them so you can take a closer look. The most common kinds are minnows.
- Crabs: these usually scuttle away as soon as you spot them, but if you're quick—and careful—you might be able to grab one. They may also be hiding in the crevices between rocks.
- Sea anemones: they may look like exotic plants, but in fact they're primitive animals related to the jellyfish. Watch out for their sting—it's best to look rather than touch.
- Starfish: these creatures crawl very slowly, using their five "arms"—they are actually more like legs, with thousands of tiny feet on the underside to enable them to move about. Their mouth is on the underside of their body.

- Limpets: try budging a limpet and you'll realize just how strong these little shellfish are, as they use a suction pad on their "foot" to stick to rock. But as soon as the tide comes in they detach themselves and move around, looking for food, before returning to exactly the same spot as before.
- Barnacles: these tiny white shellfish are usually found all over the surface of rocks—use your magnifying glass to get a good view.

sea anemone

barnacle

hermit crab

Watch the tide go in and out over the course of a day

One of the most intriguing natural phenomena is the twice-daily rhythm of the tides, and the change in the appearance of a beach between high and low tide—you would never guess that you were looking at the same place on the same day.

Tides are caused by the gravitational forces of the moon (and to a lesser extent the sun) and their pull on the vast water bodies of our planet's oceans.

Tidal height and depth vary from day to day and season to season. The biggest differences between low and high tide occur around the times of the new and full moon, when the gravitational pull of the sun adds its forces to those of the moon to create what are known as "spring tides"—though despite their name they can occur at any time of year.

When the moon is in its first or third quarter, the gravitational pull is at its weakest, and the difference between high and low tide is far less: these are known as "neap tides."

The area between high and low tides is known as the intertidal zone, which is excellent for wildlife. All kinds of marine creatures—from crabs and limpets to cockles and mussels—depend on the twice-daily changes that occur here, as do the many predators that depend on the marine life for food, especially gulls and shorebirds.

But the massive changes that occur between high and low tide don't make for an easy life—just imagine if you had to live half the day underwater and the other half exposed to the wind and sun. So the creatures that make their home between the tide lines must be tough, adaptable, and very good at hiding.

One way to appreciate the wonder of the tides is to watch the tide go in and out in the same place on the same day. You don't necessarily have to stay put all day, but you should visit three or four times during the twelve-hour tidal cycle if you can.

- Check the local times for tides where you are, either by getting hold of a set of tide tables (usually sold at seaside shops or available free at visitor information offices, or on the Internet).
- To see a really spectacular tide, check the heights and depths of the tides on your tide table. The higher and lower the figures, the greater the difference you will see.
- Try to be in position half an hour or so before high tide, then watch as the waters rise and reach their upper limit. You can mark this using a stick or a large rock.
- Then either wait and watch, or come back about three hours later, at midtide. You'll notice the difference, as your high-tide mark will now literally be high and dry.
- Return again half an hour before low tide, and when you think the tide has gone out as far as it can, put another stick or rock at the lower limit. Then pace up the beach to measure the difference between the two.
- If you have time, come back again three hours later on the rising tide, and six hours later at high tide again.

Go crabbing

There are few more satisfying vacation pastimes than sitting on the side of a harbor, dangling a length of fishing line into the water below, and feeling that sharp tug when you know you've caught a crab.

What you need

- A length of fishing line at least six yards long.
- A small weight to tie to the end of the line, to keep it under the water.
- Some bait to tie to the end of the line—crabs aren't fussy, so any piece of meat, chicken, or fish will do. Bait shops will sell you everything you need.
- A large bucket of seawater to keep the crabs in after you've caught them.

Tips

- The best places to go crabbing are seawalls, harbors, intercoastal waterways, bays, estuaries, and breakwaters with fairly deep water below. Make sure you don't fall in.
- High tide is usually the best time because the water will be deeper.
- Be patient. Crabs will sometimes take a few minutes to notice the bait, so don't keep pulling your fishing line in and out of the water.
- When you feel a sharp tug on the line, don't be tempted to pull it up straight away. Give the crab a chance to get hold of the bait, and then pull the line up slowly and carefully. At this point the crab might let go anyway, but with persistence you'll eventually manage to catch one.
- As you take it off the bait and put it in your bucket, mind the claws—they can give you a nasty bite. The best way to hold a

crab is to put your fingers and thumb on either side of its shell
and grip fairly tightly.

⚙ Take a good look at the crabs you've caught, but don't handle
them too much. Then put them carefully back into the water.

Go sea fishing

As a boy I was a typically fussy eater, and every Friday my grandmother would have a battle trying to persuade me to eat the cod,
the haddock, or the plaice she had bought from the fish delivery
van. All that changed when we went on vacation to the coast,
took a boat out, and I caught my very own mackerel.

That night our landlady cooked it for us—and for the first
time ever I cleaned my plate and asked for more. I can still
remember how incredibly fresh it tasted—so good I didn't even
mind the odd bone.

Nowadays we usually buy our fish at the supermarket, or
prepacked in frozen fillets, steaks, or fingers. But why not try
catching your own for once? Sitting down to a fish supper that
you've caught yourself is not only the freshest way to eat fish, but
it's also the most satisfying.

Most all vacation resorts on both the Pacific and Atlantic coasts—Cape Cod and the Outer Banks, Cape May, and Monterey, for example—offer sea fishing trips, with everything you need (tackle, bait, etc.) supplied. These can make a great day out for the whole family, and children often prove better than their parents at catching fish. Check out the visitor information office or the Internet, or just look out for boards advertising times and prices around the port or harbor.

Look for marine life: seabirds, seals, whales, and dolphins

The world's oceans are an amazing place: vast stretches of sea that appear so unwelcoming it's hard to believe anything could live there. But, of course, many creatures do: those birds and mammals that have adapted to survive such a harsh lifestyle.

Seeing any of these truly marine creatures—seabirds, seals, sea lions, whales, and dolphins—often means going to find them, by taking a boat out into the open ocean. But you can see others from land—if you know where and when to look. So here's a guide to help you see some of the most incredible creatures on the planet.

Manx shearwater   *puffin*   *gannet*

Seabirds

North America's coasts are home to a wide range of seabird families, ranging from gulls, jaegers, terns, and cormorants, which tend to stay close to the coast, to the true oceangoing families: shearwaters, petrels, storm petrels, gannets, and the auks, including murres, guillemots, murrelets, auklets, and puffins.

Seabirds usually nest on remote headlands or offshore islands, to avoid their eggs and chicks being eaten by predators such as squirrels, rats, and foxes. As a result, most colonies are remote and hard to reach. But you can see many seabirds—either from the shore or on a boat trip—as they pass up and down our western and eastern seaboards in spring and autumn.

Seals and sea lions

There are thirteen different kinds of seals or sea lions in North America, ranging in size from the diminutive ringed seal to the massive northern elephant seal—which weighs in at roughly six tons, roughly three times as heavy as a grizzly bear.

Slow and clumsy on land, as soon as seals and sea lions get into the water they are transformed into elegant undersea acrobats, reaching speeds of over twelve miles per hour—easily fast enough to catch their fishy prey. In comparison, the fastest human swimmer would struggle to reach a third of that speed.

The easiest way to tell seals and sea lions apart is to look at their posture on land. Seals have small front flippers that cannot support their weight, so they lie around looking rather awkward. Sea lions, also known as "eared seals," have strong front flippers, which they use to propel themselves along when ashore.

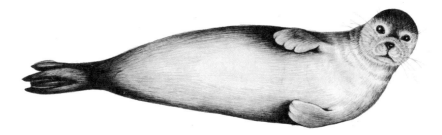

bottle-nosed dolphin

minke whale

Whales, dolphins, and porpoises

Although there are a few places where you sometimes can see whales, dolphins, and porpoises from the shore, to get really good views you usually need to take a boat trip out into the open sea.

There are quite a few companies that specialize in whale-watching trips, which can provide the experience of a lifetime. If you are really lucky you may sight gray whales, one of the great global voyagers, or even the largest animal that ever lived on the planet, the mighty blue whale.

Where to go

The best places to watch for seabirds, seals, and whales, either from the shore or on an oceangoing trip, are:

- Cape Cod, Massachusetts
- Narragansett Bay, Rhode Island
- Cape May, New Jersey
- Cape Hatteras, North Carolina
- Monterey and Big Sur, California
- San Francisco Bay, California
- Puget Sound, Washington State

Tips

- Remember, even in summer, it is always cooler at sea than on land, so wrap up warmly with a rain jacket and a fleece. Dress in layers so you can take them off or put them on as weather conditions change.
- Take plenty of sunscreen even if it's cloudy—you'll burn much more easily at sea.
- Bring binoculars and a camera.
- To avoid seasickness it's usually best to eat little and often, stay on deck, and stare at the horizon. You may want to try anti-seasick remedies, including natural ones such as ginger.
- Calm, windless days are best—not just because you're less likely to get seasick, but also because it's much easier to spot sea mammals when the surface of the sea is not too choppy.
- Cloudy days are better than sunny; glare reduces your chance of spotting a fin—but since you don't usually have much choice about the weather, you may have to take potluck!
- Look out for flocks of seabirds gathering over the water. Sea-birds mean fish, and where there are fish, there may also be whales or dolphins hunting for them.

Summer weather lore

The reason our ancestors needed proverbs and folklore to predict the summer weather was because they didn't have any proper weather forecasters, so they had to rely on a mixture of folklore and old wives' tales. Summer was a particularly crucial time of year because of the annual harvest, which, if it failed, could lead to starvation during the coming winter.

So most people looked forward to the period known as the "dog days," which begins in early July and ends in mid-August. This relates to the appearance at dawn of the brightest star in the heavens, Sirius, and is supposed to coincide with a spell of calm, settled weather, allowing the harvest to be safely gathered in.

Our ancestors also used observations of natural events, and the behavior of birds in particular, to help them forecast the weather. The habits of swallows were especially important and gave rise to a well-known proverb:

Swallows high, staying dry;
Swallows low, wet will blow.

This has a real basis in fact. Watch swallows or martins on a fine summer's evening as they hawk for insects in a darkening sky. The reason the birds are flying so high is that the insects on which they are feeding are carried up into the warm, settled air by thermal currents.

On the other hand, if the birds are flying low, it is because the air currents are being disturbed, keeping the insects low, too; and this usually signals a change to cooler, less settled weather.

So next time you see these graceful birds hunting for insects at dusk, check out where they're flying, and see what the weather is like the next day. . . .

Where swallows build their nests is also supposed to indicate the weather—this time for the whole summer season. As the old rhyme says:

When the swallow's nest is high, the summer is very dry;
When the swallow buildeth low, you can safely reap and sow.

Fall

The winds will blow their own freshness into you,
and the storms their energy,
while cares will drop away from you
like the leaves of Autumn.

—JOHN MUIR

The nights may be drawing in, and it's getting colder, but fall is still one of the best seasons to be out and about and getting back to nature. Picking berries or searching for mushrooms are just two of the many things you can do at this time of year.

Fall is a busy time for wildlife, too. With winter fast approaching, plants and animals have to take rapid action if they are going to survive the coming cold weather.

Swallows, martins, and warblers migrate, heading away from the northern regions of the United States and Canada to spend the winter in Central and South America. In their place are swans and geese on our fields and marshes. Flowers and trees are packed with fruit, nuts, and seeds, and spiders are building their webs.

But it's not all about getting ready for the winter. In the annual deer rut white-tailed deer are in the middle of their courtship season, with rival males challenging one another for the right to mate with the most females.

Fall is also a great time to make things: build a birdhouse, dig a pond, or collect some seeds and plant a tree—the fruits of your labors will pay off in the year ahead. So go on, wrap up warm, get out there, and enjoy yourself!

A note on the words we use to describe this season

The word *autumn,* which we often use in poems to describe the third season of the year, comes from the Old French—a derivation shared with the modern *automne* (French) and *otoño* (Spanish). In North America we usually use the word *fall,* brought here by English settlers in the seventeenth century. Incidentally, until the sixteenth century this season was usually simply called "harvest," the time of year when the crops are brought in from the fields.

Collect and roast sweet chestnuts

The sight of chestnuts roasting on an open fire is as American as apple pie and a white Christmas. Sadly, because of the disease known as chestnut blight (caused by a bark fungus accidentally imported from Asia), American chestnut trees are now hard to find as mature trees, with only a handful of an estimated three billion native trees remaining.

The good news is that two other species, the European sweet chestnut and the Chinese chestnut, are widely planted in North America and can be found in parks and woods in most temperate regions of the continent. Their nuts are also very tasty and can be used in all sorts of recipes.

But beware—the fruit of the imported horse chestnut tree, also known as "conkers," are poisonous, so make sure you pick the right ones. The cases of edible chestnuts are very prickly to touch, with much finer and longer spikes than those of the horse chestnut, and the nut inside has a pointed top, while the horse chestnut is much rounder and smoother.

Roasted is the nicest way to eat chestnuts, and also the simplest. Once you've collected them (any time during fall), and with an adult standing by, puncture the shell of each one with a sharp skewer or fork, or cut a cross-shaped slit across the top (to stop them from exploding; this also makes them easier to peel).

An open fire, if you have one, is the best way to roast them; the smoke gives the nuts real flavor. If not, an oven will work just as well. Just put the unpeeled chestnuts in a roasting tin and cook for half an hour or so at 400°F.

Once roasted and peeled, you can use them in cakes, stews, and soups, as the basis of Thanksgiving or Christmas turkey stuffing—or just eat them as they are.

Before chestnut blight destroyed the American chestnut in the early twentieth century, the nuts were a vital fall and winter food for all kinds of mammals and birds, including white-tailed deer, black bears, bobwhite, wild turkey, and the now extinct passenger pigeon.

The song usually known as "Chestnuts Roasting on an Open Fire" (the correct name is "The Christmas Song") was made famous by Nat King Cole. But despite its Yuletide associations, the song was actually written on a swelteringly hot summer's day in 1944, by Mel Tormé and Bob Wells.

Make jack-o'-lanterns for Halloween

Halloween, also known as All Hallows' Eve, takes place on October 31, the day before November 1, or All Saints' Day. *Hallows* means "saints."

Although nowadays Halloween is mainly associated with witches, ghouls, ghosts, or even horror movies, its true meaning is more solemn and symbolic. Its origins lie in pagan Celtic and early Christian festivals commemorating the passing of the souls of dead loved ones into the next world. This tradition is said to have been brought to North America by Irish settlers fleeing the Great Famine of the 1840s and 1850s.

One of the most enduring and familiar symbols of Halloween is the carving of pumpkins or gourds into the image of a head known as a jack-o'-lantern.

What you need

* A medium to large pumpkin—choose a nice, clean, ripe one without any bruises or cuts on the surface.
* A wax crayon or felt marker to mark out the pattern.

* A sharp, thin-bladed knife to cut the pattern. (Ask an adult to help you.)
* A large metal spoon or ice cream scoop to take out the seeds and flesh.
* A wax candle and candleholder to put inside.
* Some newspaper or other paper that you'll put under the pumpkin, so you won't mess up your mom's kitchen table or counter!

What to do

1. Cut a hole in the top of the pumpkin around the stem large enough for you to get your hand and a spoon inside (usually between half and two-thirds of the pumpkin's diameter).
2. Using a large spoon or ice cream scoop, scrape out all the flesh, until the inside walls of the pumpkin are clean and smooth.
3. With a wax crayon or felt marker, carefully trace the pattern you want to carve—a face is the usual one, but you might want to try a more abstract pattern or shape.
4. Ask an adult to cut along the pattern, then push out the pumpkin pieces for the eyes, nose, and mouth.
5. Put your candle in the candleholder and place carefully inside the pumpkin.

Pumpkins originated in the Americas, where they have been grown and eaten by native peoples for more than five thousand years. They were brought to Europe by the French explorer Jacques Cartier, who thought they were huge melons—not so far from the truth, given that pumpkins, gourds, and all members of the squash family are actually not vegetables but fruits!

Roast pumpkin seeds for a tasty snack

Roasted, salted pumpkin seeds are a tasty and nutritious snack
to keep you going on Halloween night and after. In theory they
would also be great at Christmas, but I challenge you not to have
eaten them all up by then!

What you need

* Pumpkin seeds
* Paper towel
* Cookie sheet
* Vegetable oil—sunflower works best
* Salt
* Plastic container

Here's how to make them

1. Before you throw away what you scooped out of your
   Halloween pumpkin, carefully separate the seeds from
   the pumpkin's fleshy fibers.
2. Rinse the seeds and tamp them dry with a paper towel.
3. Coat a cookie sheet lightly with vegetable oil.
4. Place the seeds in a single layer on the cookie sheet and
   sprinkle lightly with salt.
5. Bake them in the oven at 350°F for 10 to 20 minutes,
   turning them once. When they are golden and crisp they
   are ready.
6. Take them out of the oven and allow them to cool before you
   eat them.
7. To store them (if you haven't eaten them all!) put them in an
   airtight plastic container.

Apple bobbing

When I was growing up, a traditional fall activity for us kids was to tour the neighborhood looking for apple trees on the edges of gardens. When we found one, we would shinny up the wall or climb up the tree and pick them—an activity we called scrumping. This was, of course, technically against the law, though there is also another tradition, known as usufruct, which refers to the right to use someone else's property so long as it is not damaged—so perhaps taking the odd apple is OK after all!

A more wholesome pastime, also associated with Halloween, is apple bobbing. This simple game originated in the Celtic cultures of Scotland and Ireland and is associated with the pagan festival of Samhain (a forerunner of Halloween).

The rules are simple

✳ Fill up a bowl or basin with water, and float apples on the surface.
✳ Each player then tries to pick up as many apples as he or she can in a limited amount of time—using only their teeth! Hands should be placed (or tied) behind the back to prevent cheating!

It is sometimes said that the first person to successfully pick up the apple will also be the first in the group to get married; if a girl places the apple she has picked up beneath her pillow she is said to dream of her future husband.

Watch birds feeding on fruit and berries

Birds love berries—especially in the fall, when they need to build up their energy levels to be ready for the coming cold weather or for migration. But berries love birds, too—or at least the trees and bushes that produce them do.

That's because after a bird has eaten a berry, and taken all the goodness from the fleshy pulp around the seeds, those seeds come out the other end of the bird. And because birds travel, the seeds may be dropped a long way from wherever they were eaten—enabling the parent plant to spread into new areas.

That's why berries look so delicious. The bright colors (especially red) have evolved to entice birds to feed on them; and the soft flesh of an elderberry or blackberry is the bird's reward for helping to spread those precious seeds. A word of warning, though: some delicious-looking berries can be eaten by birds but are poisonous to us.

Over generations, birds and berry-bearing plants have grown to depend on each other. Thrushes, waxwings, and robins in particular need a good berry crop in order to survive the winter—and this provides us with the ideal opportunity to watch the birds at close quarters.

So as soon as the weather turns colder in fall, stake out a berry bush and watch what comes to feed. Likely species are the cedar waxwing, rose-breasted or evening grosbeak, eastern or western kingbirds, and the American robin. Watch how these birds will often defend their bush and its precious berries against any intruders.

If you want to plant trees and shrubs to produce berries for birds, here are some useful tips.

* For summer berries, plant elderberry, blueberry, and service-berry (also known as Juneberry).
* For fall and winter berries, plant dogwood, bayberry, holly, and snowberry.
* Try to avoid invasive exotic plants such as Japanese honey-suckle, Chinese and Japanese privets, European buckthorn, and white mulberry; they may spread from your garden and cause problems in your neighborhood.

How to identify . . .
coastal birds

Most of North America's nine hundred or so different species of bird are landlubbers, who rarely, if ever, catch sight of the sea. Others, like the shearwaters and petrels, are truly pelagic—that is, they spend their lives out in the open ocean.

But others—notably gulls and terns, but also loons, gannets, pelicans, and skimmers—live their lives on that dividing line between land and sea, the coast. So whichever coast you visit, from Seattle to Los Angeles and from New England to Florida, you can be sure you'll catch sight of at least some of these adaptable and fascinating birds.

How to identify . . .
coastal birds

Northern gannet
A large, distinctive seabird with a mainly white plumage, yellowish head, and sharp, daggerlike bill. In flight it shows black wingtips. Youngsters are much darker brown in color.

Common loon
This legendary bird, revered by many Native American peoples for its mythical powers, mainly nests on our northern lakes and ponds. But from fall to spring, loons can be seen off our coasts. Look out for a large, low-swimming bird with a dark plumage and heavy bill.

Brown pelican
A common sight along many of our coasts, the adult brown pelican is easily identified by its large size, all-dark plumage (apart from a paler head), and huge bill. Sociable—often seen diving for fish in large flocks.

American white pelican
The larger of our two pelicans, and with its huge size, all-white plumage, huge yellow bill, and black flight feathers, it is impossible to mistake for any other bird. Found along all our coasts but commoner in the West and Gulf of Mexico.

Double-crested cormorant
The commonest of our six cormorant species, identified by its distinctive orange-yellow bill and chin. Often perches with wings outstretched in order to dry them. Found on all coasts and often inland, too.

Herring gull
Our commonest and most widespread large gull, with a pale gray back, white below, pinkish legs, and yellow bill spotted with red. Youngsters are mainly brown. Common along all coasts and inland.

Black skimmer
A bizarre-looking bird the size of a large tern, black above, white below, with a huge orange-red bill tipped with black. The lower bill is longer than the upper, allowing the bird to fish by dipping the lower bill into the water and snapping shut when it catches a fish! Mainly found along the Atlantic and Gulf coasts.

Laughing gull
Commonest of our "black-hooded" gulls, especially along the Atlantic and Gulf coasts, where it is often the only gull present in large numbers. In summer it has a dark head and red bill, dark gray back, and white below. In winter it loses its black hood and becomes duskier below; its bill turns black.

Common tern
Classic medium-size tern: elegant and slender, with a buoyant flight and obvious forked tail. Adults are pale gray above, white below, with red bill tipped with black. Common along all our coasts.

California gull
Medium-size gull with light gray back, pale below, yellow legs, and streaking on the back of the neck. Breeds on the Great Plains and is also found all along the Pacific Coast, but very rare in the the eastern United States.

Collect pinecones and make them into Christmas decorations

Pinecones are little miracles of nature—each one can hold hundreds of tiny seeds, protected against hungry predators until the cone opens and releases the seeds into the wind. Cones from pines—and from other conifers such as spruces, larches, and firs—have a long tradition of being made into children's toys and Christmas decorations such as wreaths.

In parts of Scandinavia, pinecones are often turned into "cone cows"—just push in sticks or matches for legs! Another simple way to make an attractive seasonal decoration for fall or winter is to spray the cones different colors using aerosol paint— just be careful not to breathe too deeply when you are spraying, and put paper down first to avoid making a mess!

Go on a "fungal foray"

Fungi are bizarre things. Neither plant nor animal, they are among the largest living creatures on the planet, stretching for miles underground. But the only part of this vast organism we see is its fruit: the mushrooms and toadstools that appear—as if by magic—in our forests and fields every fall.

Many people are put off searching for fungi because they're worried about being poisoned. But as long as you're careful and sensible—and don't pick or eat any fungus you aren't absolutely sure of—you will be perfectly safe. If you aren't confident about whether a mushroom is poisonous or not, then don't touch it.

To discover more about our fascinating fungi, why not go on a "fungal foray"—either on your own or on an organized walk with an expert to guide you? Many local wildlife groups run these events during the fall months. You'll be amazed at the hidden secrets behind these weird and wonderful organisms. . . .

When to go

Fungi generally appear in the fall, and the best time to look for them is early in the morning on a mild day from September through early November, depending on where you live.

Where to go

Fungi can be found almost anywhere—though they prefer damp places where they can obtain precious nutrients from the soil or from other decaying material such as rotten trees.

Forests are always a good place to look. Many kinds of fungi, such as the bracket fungus, actually grow on trees. The edges of fields and open glades in woods are also fungal hot spots. You may even get some growing in your backyard.

What to take

* Gloves, if you want to handle fungi.
* A field guide to help you identify what you find.
* A digital camera to take pictures of the fungi.
* A small container if you plan to collect a few specimens.

What's the difference between a mushroom and a toadstool?

* There isn't one. However, we generally use the term "toadstool" to refer to poisonous fungi, and "mushroom" for those we can eat.

Fungi have some really odd names—look at these for starters:

* Shaggy mane—looks like a folded umbrella.
* Parasol mushroom—resembles an open umbrella!

- Oyster mushroom—shaped like an oyster shell.
- Old man of the woods—cap turns black, then gray with age.
- Bird's nest fungus—looks exactly like a clutch of eggs inside a cup.
- Orange peel—evokes the discarded skin of an orange.
- Sulphur shelf—named after its bright orange-yellow color and flat appearance. Its other name, chicken-of-the-woods, comes from its flavor when cooked.
- And a host of poisonous fungi, with gruesome names including death cup, fly agaric, false morel, and hemlock polypore.

There are all sorts of bizarre beliefs and old wives' tales about how to tell a poisonous fungus from an edible one. These include the idea that any mushroom that peels is edible (wrong); that all mushrooms collected from fields are edible (wrong); or that if you boil a mushroom with a silver spoon, and the spoon turns black, the mushroom is poisonous (also wrong).

Collect seeds and plant them

Collecting seeds—then planting them—is one of the best ways to learn about how nature works. It's also easy to do and good fun. You can start by collecting seeds from plants in your backyard or local park; then look for tree seeds such as acorns, beechnuts, or pinecones, and plant a tree.

Collecting flower seeds

From late summer into autumn, many wildflowers begin to set seed, ensuring that the following spring and summer the countryside will once again be awash with color as they come into bloom. You can be part of this natural cycle by collecting flower seeds for yourself, planting them, and watching them grow.

When to go

Most plants set seed in late summer and early fall, so this is the ideal time for seed collecting. Good ones to collect include poppies, cornflowers, and nasturtiums.

What to do

* Look for plants whose flowers have already fallen off and where the seed heads are showing.
* Check for ripeness: if the seed heads are still green they aren't ready yet; if they've turned brown and rattle when you shake them, they are.
* Pick the seed heads and put them in an envelope—use a different envelope for each kind of plant. Write the name of the plant on the outside of the envelope.
* Leave them somewhere warm and dry.
* When the seed heads are completely dry, shake them over a piece of paper so the seeds fall out. You may need to sift them to get rid of the chaff.
* Then place the seeds back in the envelope until the spring, when it's time to plant them.

Collecting tree seeds

Visiting a forest in fall to collect tree seeds is a great day out for all the family. All you need is something to put the seeds in and a guide to recognizing which seeds come from which tree.

Good seeds to look for and collect are

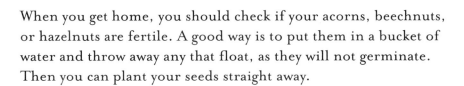

* Beechnuts.
* Hazelnuts.
* Acorns (from oak trees).
* Chinese or sweet chestnuts.
* Seeds from alder cones or strobiles.
* Seeds from pinecones.

When you get home, you should check if your acorns, beechnuts, or hazelnuts are fertile. A good way is to put them in a bucket of water and throw away any that float, as they will not germinate. Then you can plant your seeds straight away.

What you need

* Some containers for growing (buy at your local garden center, or just use old flowerpots).
* Compost and soil to grow them in.
* Labels to mark the containers so you know which seed is which.

What to do

* Fill your container with a mixture of compost and soil, and then plant your seeds—nuts and acorns should be sown an inch or so below the surface, while alder and pine seeds can be sown almost at the top.

* Once you've planted each seed make sure you write a label so you don't forget what you've sown. Water them, then leave the containers in a cool, shady spot (a shed or garage is ideal) until the spring.
* By springtime the seeds should have begun to germinate, and you will have a tiny plant in each container. Water them carefully—not too much, or they'll get too wet, but enough to stop them from drying out.
* When they are about nine to twelve inches tall it's time to plant them—find a suitable spot in the corner of your backyard, but don't put them too close together. Clearing weeds away and putting some mulch or compost around the base will help them grow.

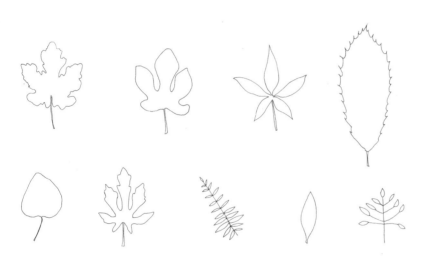

Make leaf rubbings

Making leaf rubbings is a classic fall activity that, like so many other traditional outdoor pastimes, has declined in recent years. Yet it's one of the easiest ways to create your own wrapping paper or gift cards.

First, visit a local park or woodland and collect a range of different fallen leaves. If you can, make a note of which leaf came from which kind of tree.

Then, make leaf rubbings

* Once your leaf has completely dried out, place it upside down on a piece of board (with the veins facing upward).
* Place a piece of white or colored paper on top, and holding it down firmly, rub the paper with a pencil, crayon, or piece of charcoal.
* You will start to see the pattern of the leaf appear on the paper. Make sure you rub over the whole of the leaf, and then lift the paper off.
* You can make different-colored patterns or use different leaves to make a pattern, then paste into a scrapbook or hang up on the wall or fridge door. Or cut around the edge of the leaf rubbing and use in a collage (see below).

Other things you can do with leaves

LEAF PRINTS
Using a paint roller, spread paint smoothly over the surface of the leaf, making sure it is completely covered. Then turn the leaf over and press it firmly onto the surface of some plain white or colored paper. Hang it up to dry, and you have a leaf print.

LEAF COLLAGES
Glue the leaves (or your leaf rubbings) onto white or colored paper to form patterns. Try overlapping them to form 3-D layers, or use different-colored leaves to create shapes and patterns. Once your collage is finished, put it under a pile of books so the leaves dry and stay stuck to the paper.

LEAF T-SHIRTS

You can do your leaf collage on a plain white T-shirt, using special fabric paint, so you can wash the T-shirt when it gets dirty, then hang it up to dry.

Listen for owls calling

Although owls hoot throughout the year, fall nights are often a good time to listen for them, as very few other birds are singing.

To listen for owls, choose a calm, windless night between September and November, ideally when it's cold and clear. Owls hate rain as much as we do! Wait until darkness falls, then visit a local forest. You can wander about, but you're more likely to hear the birds, and be able to work out where the sounds are coming from, if you stand still.

Once you hear the hooting, move toward the source of the sound. But take care—you don't want to frighten the birds. Then just close your eyes and listen to one of the great natural sounds.

If you can, try to identify the species you are listening to. Here are some ways to tell them apart:

* Barred owl: "Who cooks for you? Who cooks for you all?"
* Great horned owl: deep, muffled, and rhythmic—"Hoo-hoohoo-hoo."
* Northern spotted owl: rhythmic, barking sound—"Whuupp, hoo-hoo."
* Barn owl: hissing shriek—which explains its alternative name of "screech owl."
* Eastern screech owl: sounds like a whinnying horse!

Tip

Cup your hands behind your ears and stand facing the direction where the call is coming from. This will amplify the sound and help you pinpoint where the owl is sitting. This works well with any birdsong, so you can try it out in spring as well.

Look for spiders in your house

Fall is a very good time to look for spiders—or a very bad time, if you're scared of them!

At this time of year they can turn up anywhere: on the living room carpet, on your quilt, or of course in the bath. By the way, it's a myth that spiders crawl up the drain; once they've fallen in, they can't climb up the slippery sides without a helping hand from us.

Another spider found in many of our homes, but often overlooked, is the daddy longlegs spider. It's called that because it looks just like the insect known as the "daddy longlegs" (called the crane fly in the southeastern United States) and also the harvestman (also, confusingly, known as "daddy longlegs").

This harmless and unobtrusive creature sits quite still in an untidy, tangled web in the corner of a room, where the ceiling meets the wall. Until you take a closer look, you will probably think the web is empty, as the spider that lives there is so thin and weedy it's very hard to spot.

But take a pencil and give the web a gentle prod, and the spider suddenly starts to vibrate rapidly up and down—its way of fooling other spiders that might make a meal of it. If attacked, the spider will also use its long legs to throw strands of web at the intruder to fend it off.

By sitting so quietly in what looks like a few tangled bits of web, the daddy longlegs spider catches many an unwary insect, and it will even eat other spiders, including its own kind. The offspring keep out of one another's way, too, for fear that they might be munched by a sibling.

The daddy longlegs spider is not native to North America—it originated in the tropics.

It is sometimes said that the daddy longlegs spider is the most poisonous creature on the planet, and that if its jaws were able to pierce human skin it could kill us in seconds. Fortunately, this is completely untrue.

Look for spiderwebs on a fall morning

A fine morning in fall is the ideal time to go looking for spiderwebs. If it's cold and clear, dew will form along the individual strands, making them easier to see. Try standing behind a web as it is backlit by the rays of the early-morning sun—truly magical!

Amazing facts about spiders and their webs

* There are at least forty thousand different kinds of spiders in the world—of which well over three thousand are found in North America.
* The silk spiders use to make their webs is—weight for weight—stronger than steel.
* A typical web is made of strands of silk about $1/5000$th of an inch across.

* If you look really closely at a spiderweb you'll see little blobs of a sticky, gluelike substance, which the spider uses to catch its prey.
* Some male spiders twang their webs like a guitar to attract a mate.
* When a fly or other insect lands in a web, the spider can tell where the insect is by feeling its movements through the strands of the web.

Another thing to look out for at this time of year is the natural phenomenon known as gossamer. These are the fine silken threads that appear, as if by magic, draped across bushes and grass on fresh, clear fall mornings.

Gossamer is actually spun by tiny baby spiders (also known as "spiderlings"). They then launch themselves into the air, and in a process known as "ballooning," float away on individual lines of web to find a new place to live.

These delicate but incredibly strong strands enable the spiderlings to travel vast distances—several hundred miles away, and up to two miles above the ground—in the space of a single day.

The word gossamer *is thought to come from the phrase "goose summer," and derives from the mistaken belief that these fine strands of silk that appeared at this time of year were actually goose down.*

Make a woodpile in your backyard

This will create a hidden haven for wild creatures such as wood lice, bumblebees, frogs and newts, mice, stag beetles, and maybe even snakes and lizards, as well as a range of lichens and fungi.

What to do

* Go to a local park or forest and look for logs and dead branches.
* Bring them home and pile them up in a quiet corner of your yard—ideally somewhere shady and a bit damp, such as under trees or shrubs.
* Wait for the wildlife to arrive. . . .

A stag beetle spends up to seven years underground in the form of a larva before pu-
pating in autumn, and emerging the following summer as a flying adult. Adult stag
beetles enjoy their freedom for just a few weeks: fighting, mating, laying eggs, and
then dying before the summer is over. In medieval England, peasants believed that
stag beetles had the power to summon thunder and lightning, and carried hot coals
in their jaws, dropping them to set fire to buildings.

How to identify . . .
small mammals

Small mammals are among the commonest creatures in North America—yet are also often very difficult to see. Even when you do catch a glimpse of them, it is usually just the sight of a rapidly disappearing furry rear end. There are three main groups of small mammals: bats, rodents (squirrels, chipmunks, rats, mice, and voles), and insectivores (shrews). Some, like chipmunks, are easier to see than others, but if you want to get really good views, you may have to be patient!

How to identify . . .
small mammals

Red squirrel
Found mainly in our northern and mountain forests, this attractive little squirrel is full of energy, especially early and late in the day. Dark reddish brown above; white below; with a bushy tail often held above its body.

Masked shrew
One of our commonest mammals, found right across the northern states, though missing from the South. Yet because of the masked (or common) shrew's small size and secretive nature, it is hardly ever seen. If you do see it, look out for its gray-brown color, long snout and tail, and rapid movements.

Eastern gray squirrel
The commonest squirrel in the eastern United States, coming in various shades of gray and brown (those in parts of Canada and some other northern areas are black). A common resident of parks, suburban backyards, and forests.

Little brown bat
North America's commonest bat, found everywhere apart from the extreme South, and often seen in towns and cities. Small (about four inches long with a wingspan of eight to ten inches), with a low, erratic flight.

Flying squirrels

The northern and southern flying squirrels are both small, plump rodents with the ability to glide through the air using wide flaps of skin along their sides. Unlike other North American squirrels, flying squirrels are mainly nocturnal.

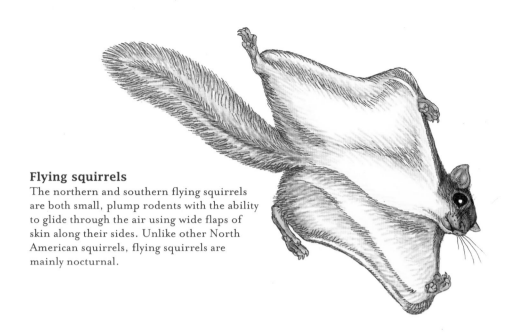

Deer mouse

One of the most widespread small mammals in North America, found everywhere apart from the southeastern states of the United States. Mainly nocturnal, with large ears and eyes and a white belly.

Meadow vole

Also known (inaccurately) as the field mouse, this is a medium-size, plump rodent with the short ears and short tail characteristic of its family. Very common on grasslands throughout much of North America, and an important food for all kinds of creatures, including birds of prey.

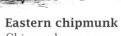

Eastern chipmunk

Chipmunks are a group of squirrels living mainly on the ground rather than in trees, and nesting in underground burrows. Eastern chipmunks have the characteristic white stripes, bordered with black, along their sides and face.

Trap small mammals

Although birds are the most visible wild creatures, small mammals are just as common.

But if that's the case, why do we hardly ever see them? One reason is that many are nocturnal. Another is that small mammals such as mice and voles are eaten by all sorts of other creatures, from owls and hawks to coyotes and foxes. So they sensibly stay out of sight—which means we have to use special methods to see them: small-mammal traps.

Small-mammal traps shouldn't really be used unless you're trained to use them and are experienced at handling whatever you catch. So the best way to experience mammal trapping is to go along with an expert, who can show you the tricks of the trade without causing the animals any harm.

Many local conservation groups run mammal-trapping events from spring through summer to autumn. They use specially baited traps that attract the animal and keep it fed while it is waiting for the trapper to release it. They are also filled with bedding material so the animal can keep warm.

Traps should be checked frequently, as it is important that the animal is not left there for more than a few hours at most.

Observe deer during the rutting season

The annual deer rut—when the dominant males defend their harem of females against rival stags and bucks—is one of our great natural spectacles. Watching a buck deer bellowing at another, before engaging in head-to-head combat with those clashing antlers, is an unforgettable experience. It's also surprisingly easy to see—provided you get the timing right.

When to go

The white-tailed deer and mule deer ruts usually occur from
October through November, though the exact time will vary,
depending on the location and the weather conditions that particular year.

Early mornings and evenings are the best times; not only are
the deer more active but the light is also usually better.

Fine, cold days also generally see more activity and provide
better conditions for watching the rut.

Tips

* To find rutting deer, listen and smell as well as look. Listen
  for their roaring sounds; look for areas where the deer have
  scraped the ground; and see if you can smell the distinctive
  scent they emit at this time of year.
* Be very quiet, and move slowly and carefully—you don't want
  to frighten the animals you've come to see. Deer have phe-
  nomenal hearing, so take only a few steps at a time as you
  move from tree to tree.
* Don't go too close—if a rutting buck sees you he will probably
  run away.
* If you're looking for wild deer, wear camouflage clothing and
  hide behind trees to break up your silhouette, since they are
  very wary.

Make a birdhouse

Making a birdhouse isn't as difficult as you might think. You don't need to be an expert carpenter. All you need is some wood, the right tools, and a bit of persistence.

Basic tools and equipment

* A plank of wood, about four to five feet long, six to eight inches wide, and about ¾ inch thick.
* A sharp wood saw.
* Galvanized nails, panel pins, or wood screws.
* A strip of leather, rubber, or heavy-duty carpet tape.
* A hook and eye to make the lid secure from predators.
* A power drill, with a suitably sized cutting blade for making the entrance hole.
* A tape measure.

Because this involves a lot of drilling (using power tools), it's best to ask an adult to do this for you.

1. Mark out the plank with the shapes of your birdhouse. The back panel can vary in size, depending on where you want to fix it, but it must be at least ten inches long.
2. Ask an adult to cut the wood into six pieces, being careful to keep the cuts straight and at right angles to the edge of the plank. The exception to this is the cut between the two side pieces, which should be made at a shallow angle.
3. Drill two small holes at the top and bottom of the back panel, so that once you've finished making the birdhouse you'll be able to fix it to a fence, wall, or tree.
4. Nail or screw the two side panels to the base.
5. Drill a hole in the front panel, about five inches from the bottom. The hole can vary in size from about 1 inch, for smaller birds such as chickadees, to about 1⅓ inches for larger birds, such as sparrows.

6. Drill a few small holes in the base so that water can drain away if the birdhouse gets flooded in heavy rain.
7. Nail or screw the base and front panel to the birdhouse.
8. Fix the roof, using a strip of leather, rubber, or carpet tape to make a hinge. Make the lid secure with a hook and eye.
9. Before you put your birdhouse up, waterproof the outside with a wood-preserving agent such as creosote. Never put this on the inside of the birdhouse: it may harm the birds.

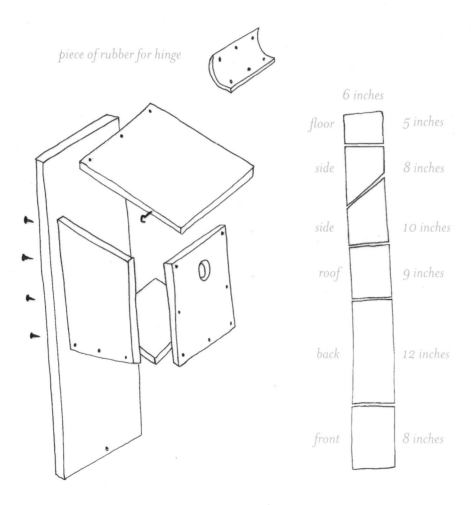

piece of rubber for hinge

6 inches

floor — *5 inches*

side — *8 inches*

side — *10 inches*

roof — *9 inches*

back — *12 inches*

front — *8 inches*

Don't worry if your birdhouse looks a bit crooked, or doesn't match up to the ones in a store. Remember that natural nest sites in walls and trees don't come in a regular shape or size, yet the birds are still happy to use them.

Putting up your birdhouse

When you're deciding where to place your birdhouse, there are a few basic rules to follow.

* Put it up in fall or early winter, so the birds have a chance to get used to it before the breeding season begins.
* Affix it to a tree, wall, or garden fence at least five feet above the ground. Use large nails or screws if you're attaching it to a post or fence, or hang it from a wire if you're suspending it from a tree.
* Make sure the birdhouse faces away from direct sunlight, preferably somewhere between north and southeast.
* Try to tilt the front of the birdhouse downward a little, to keep out the rain.
* If you're putting up several birdhouses, keep them some distance apart, to stop rival males from fighting each other over disputed territory.

Once your birdhouse is up, be patient. Garden birds often take a while to get used to one, and you may have to wait a whole year before they venture inside and make it their home. And when they do, try not to check it out too often—it may disturb the birds and cause them to desert their eggs.

Finally, every fall, when you are absolutely sure all the young have left home, it's time for a good cleaning. Throw away any old nesting material, and then thoroughly scrub down the birdhouse, using hot water and dishwashing soap. Don't use any other household chemicals; they may harm the birds that will occupy it next year.

Dig a pond in your backyard

It has been said that a wildlife yard without a pond is like a theater without a stage. And it's certainly true that even the smallest pond will make your backyard more attractive to wild-life.

By providing somewhere for birds and mammals to drink and bathe, for amphibians and insects to lay their eggs, and for flowers and aquatic plants to grow, you'll also be able to enjoy watching a whole new world of wild creatures.

What you need

* Bamboo poles or rope to outline the shape of your pond.
* Spades to dig out the soil, and a wheelbarrow to take it away.
* A tape measure and calculator to determine what size lining you will need.
* Old blankets or carpet to protect the lining against sharp objects.
* Butyl rubber lining—you can get this from your local garden center.
* A sharp knife or heavy-duty scissors—but make sure an adult is there to help you use them.
* Stones or rocks to keep the lining in place.
* Sand.

What to do

* Starting from the middle, in terms of both length and width, dig your hole.
* Make sure you vary the depth to provide shallow and deep areas—between one and two and a half feet deep is ideal (once the lining is in, this will make a pond between four inches and two feet deep).
* Remove any sharp rocks and stones and add a layer of sand.
* Put the old blankets or carpets on top of the sand, then the lining on top of those.
* Put in another layer of sand.
* Fill the pond with a hose; then add a bucketful of water from another pond.
* Your pond is ready to go. . . .

It may not look like much, but if you add some aquatic plants (ask at a garden center for advice on which ones), it will start to take shape. Ideally you want a combination of submerged, floating, and edge-based plants—marsh marigold, water lilies, and yellow iris are ideal.

Top tips

* Don't put in fish. Fishponds and wildlife ponds don't really go together, since fish tend to eat the wildlife.
* Don't take plants from the wild.
* Keep the surface of your pond tidy, removing leaves in fall and algae in summer.
* If young children (four years old and below) visit the garden, then make sure the pond is securely covered so they can't fall in.

Plant a native hedgerow in your backyard

Hedgerows are a common sight in the English countryside, where they traditionally formed the boundary between farm fields, though they are less frequently found in the United States. They come in all shapes and sizes, but the best for wildlife is a hedgerow made up of native plants, which will provide food and shelter for a whole range of garden creatures. A hedgerow is easy to plant and will provide a refuge for wild-life—as well as an attractive feature for your backyard—in just a couple of years.

When to plant

The best time to plant your hedge is during the late fall, between October and November (if the ground isn't already frozen!), when hedgerow plants are dormant. Don't plant if the ground is waterlogged or there's a heavy frost.

What to plant

Choose native species of hedgerow plants, small trees such as American hazel, dogwood, maple, and wild plum. These are available from specialized nurseries or mail-order suppliers, who will also be able to give you advice on when and how to plant your hedge.

How to plant

* ❋ Decide where you want to put the hedgerow, and clear all weeds from the soil to a width of about one yard, and to the length you want the hedgerow to be.
* ❋ Spread a layer of compost or manure pellets across the area to a depth of about two inches.
* ❋ Plant two rows of one or two plants every foot or so, each row about twelve to eighteen inches apart, staggering the plants along each row.
* ❋ Add another thick layer of mulch.
* ❋ Once your hedgerow is in, try to keep the area around it free from weeds to allow the plants to grow.
* ❋ If you have pets or animals, such as rabbits, that might eat the hedge, protect it with wire or fencing, especially in the first couple of years, when the young plants are most vulnerable.

How to identify . . .
medium-size mammals

This group includes some of North America's most familiar, widespread, and best-known creatures. Some, like the red fox and racoon, have adapted to living in our towns and cities to take advantage of the food we waste in our trash cans. Others, like the snowshoe hare, live in remote, mountainous areas and can be very hard to see.

Many mammals are more active either at night, or at dawn and dusk, so these are good times to go and look for them. Be aware that many have excellent eyesight and hearing—but that one of the main ways they detect intruders in their territory is by smell. So always try to keep quiet, dress in muted colors, and stay downwind of them—otherwise they will soon realize you are there and be away in a flash!

How to identify . . .
medium-size mammals

Fisher
This large weasel in the same family as the American marten is found mainly in the northern states of the United States, where it lives in wooded habitats along rivers, hunting for small mammals, birds, and reptiles. Very dark, with small ears and head and bushy tail.

Red fox
Known for its intelligence and cunning, the red fox lives in a wide range of habitats and has adapted well to living in our suburban and city neighborhoods, where there is plenty of food available from our wasteful habits. Reddish brown above and white below, with pointed ears and a bushy tail.

Porcupine
This extraordinary animal—actually a large, nocturnal rodent—defends itself against predators by turning its back on them and displaying its thirty thousand or so sharp, pointed quills. Found mainly in the North and West, mainly in forests, where they feed on bark and the new growth of trees.

Raccoon
One of the few North American animals to benefit from the growth of the human population, the raccoon has quickly adapted to living in our neighborhoods, where it obtains much of its food by scavenging in trash cans. Its bushy tail and masked appearance make it easy to identify.

Northern river otter
This beautiful creature of our rivers and streams is one of the very few animals at home on both land and water. Its long, slender body (up to four and a half feet, including the tail), small ears, and midbrown fur distinguish it from the smaller, darker mink.

Jackrabbit
Jackrabbits—actually a kind of hare—are among our fastest mammals, able to flee from predators at an incredible 35 miles per hour. Like other hares they do not dig burrows, but rest in shallow depressions in the ground known as "forms."

Badger

A strong and sometimes aggressive animal, the badger can be easily identified by its black-and-white head pattern, short legs, and long snout. Found mainly in dry plains and prairies, especially in the western United States.

Eastern cottontail

The commonest rabbit east of the Rockies, this is the classic rabbit: brown fur, short legs, long ears, and the fluffy, white tail that gives this rabbit its name—often seen as the animal runs away from you!

Striped skunk

One of North America's most notorious animals, with its ability to spray foul-smelling fluid over any predator or intruder—including us! Mainly black, with characteristic white stripes along its back and large, fluffy tail.

Snowshoe hare

This plump, short-eared, and large-footed hare is famous for its ability to change its appearance to suit the season. In spring and summer they are the brown color typical of hares and rabbits; but as autumn arrives they begin to turn white, enabling them to be camouflaged in the winter snow.

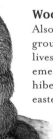

Woodchuck

Also known, famously, as the groundhog, this plump rodent lives in a system of burrows, emerging in spring after a long hibernation. Found in the northeastern United States.

Nine-banded armadillo

A classic creature of the southeastern United States, this bizarre-looking animal is, as its name suggests, covered in a hard, bony shell. Lives in underground burrows, which it digs with its powerful claws, and uses its long, sticky tongue to capture ants and termites from their colonies.

Beaver

Well known for their ability to build dams by felling trees with those sharp teeth and powerful jaws, beavers are found in lakes, rivers, and streams throughout North America. A large mammal (some are more than three feet long), with brown, shaggy fur and a paddle-shaped tail, which can add up to another foot to their length.

Be blown by the wind

When the wind blows really hard—especially during fall—find an exposed spot on a high hill and just allow yourself to be blown around by its mighty force. Wonderful!

Fall weather lore

No warmth, no cheerfulness, no healthful ease,
No comfortable feel in any member,
No shade, no shine, no butterflies, no bees,
No fruits, no flowers, no leaves, no birds,
No-vember.
—THOMAS HOOD

Fall can be a pretty miserable time of year, weather-wise, as Thomas Hood's poem suggests. And it has also given rise to all sorts of verses, proverbs, and old wives' tales about the weather, many of which come from our observations of nature.

Some suggest that wild creatures know when the coming winter will be a hard one and therefore make certain they get enough to eat to survive a cold spell: "When birds are fat in October, expect a cold winter."

Mist or fog, on the other hand, is good news—especially early on a fall morning, meaning fine weather to come that day.

You can also observe the behavior of familiar wild animals and see if you can predict the weather this way, as in the following beliefs.

* If geese or other waterbirds are seen heading out to sea, fine weather is meant to be on the way; but if they head inland, bad weather is due.
* With domestic geese, the thickness of their bones (presumably after being killed, cooked, and eaten!) is also supposed to forecast the severity of the coming winter—thick bones foretell a harsh winter.
* The thickness of the brown bands on the woolly bear caterpillar (the larva of the Isabella tiger moth, a common species across much of the United States) is also supposed to foretell a harsh winter—the wider the bands, the colder the winter. However, even in the same brood the thickness of the bands varies considerably, so this prediction must be taken with a large grain of salt!

Indeed, any fall weather forecast that claims to use animals' appearance or behavior to predict long-term weather for the coming winter or next spring is likely to be utter baloney—though we can but hope. . . .

Winter

Now winter nights enlarge
The number of their hours,
And clouds their storms discharge
Upon the airy towers.

Let now the chimneys blaze,
And cups o'erflow with wine;
Let well-tuned words amaze
With harmony divine.

—THOMAS CAMPION, "NOW WINTER NIGHTS ENLARGE"

Of all the seasons, winter may seem the least promising—at least when it comes to being out in the natural world. Surely it's better to stay indoors, open our holiday presents, and wait until the coming of spring?

On the other hand, after too much food and drink during the festive season, it's always good to dress up warmly and go out for a walk—a great way to clear away the cobwebs and breathe in some fresh air.

And although things are quieter in winter from a wildlife point of view, there are still things to see and do—provided you know where to look. Woods and forests may seem empty, but with patience you can hear the high-pitched calls of small birds in search of food.

Beaches are great places for a winter walk, too—and if you feel really tough, why not have a swim in the sea? It's warmer than you might think! If you head for open water—either inland or on the coast—there should be flocks of wildfowl and shorebirds battling to survive against the winter cold.

It's obvious that in recent years things have changed. In some parts of the United States winter weather patterns have altered a lot—which may mean you get less snow than you used to in your neighborhood. Although you might not always be able to build a snowman or have snowball fights, there may be new opportunities to see winter wildlife.

Feed the ducks

Is there anyone who hasn't fed the ducks at least once in their lives? For many of us—including me—it's the very first encounter with nature we had as a young child. So if you're planning to visit your town or city park, here are some tips on what to do.

* Although white bread doesn't do ducks much good, it won't do them any real harm either. But avoid it if you can—wholemeal bread is better.
* If you want to feed the ducks regularly and are prepared to spend a bit more to give them something more nutritious, then buy seeds or grains from a reputable bird-food supplier.
* For a real show, throw small bits of bread up into the air and watch the gulls swoop down and catch a piece before it hits the water. You can play a game with your friends and family— who can get the highest number of catches with ten pieces of bread?

Coots and moorhens may look like ducks, act like ducks, and even sound a bit like ducks, but they're not related at all. They're actually members of the rail family that have adapted to life on the water. Next time you see one, take a look at its bill (short and pointed rather than long and flat) and its feet (long toes with tiny webs rather than fully webbed), and you'll see the difference.

How to identify . . .
ducks and waterbirds

We all love feeding the ducks, and it's another really good way to get to know a range of different birds. Your local park pond is a good place to start; you can also visit a river, lake, or marsh—any large area of water will be home to a good range of the birds featured here.

Most ducks come in two plumages: male and female. The male is usually brightly colored, while the female is duller—because she does all the incubating duties and needs to be camouflaged to avoid being seen by predators.

But ducks aren't the only waterbirds you are likely to see. There are also swans and geese—both closely related to ducks—and elegant, long-legged herons and egrets; as well as coots and kingfishers.

How to identify . . .
ducks and waterbirds

Canada goose

As its name suggests, the Canada goose breeds in the far north but is often seen on migration or on its wintering grounds farther south. Very distinctive, with combination of brown plumage, blackish brown neck, and white cheek patches.

Great blue heron

North America's largest heron, standing almost four feet tall and with a six-foot wingspan. Bluish gray in color, the adults have a yellow bill and black plumes on the head. Found in suitable wetland habitats throughout the United States.

Mute swan

Introduced from Europe, this is one of our largest, heaviest, and most distinctive birds. Adults are white, with yellow on the neck and a deep orange and black bill. Can be aggressive if you approach them closely, especially when they have eggs or chicks to look after.

Brant

One of our smallest geese, the various races of the brant are Arctic breeders but then head south to overwinter in coastal areas of the United States. Very dark, with all-black head, white necklace, dark gray belly (varies depending on the race), and white under the tail.

Wood duck

Our most beautiful duck—at least the male is, with his extraordinary array of colors ranging from green through red, yellow and blue, and his distinctive crest. Female is much duller—basically gray-brown, with a white patch around her eye. Commoner in the eastern United States and northern Pacific states.

Snowy egret

This elegant, snow-white bird is one of our most attractive waterbirds, especially when seen hunting, stalking its prey of fish or frogs before stabbing with that sharp, daggerlike bill. Commoner in the southern United States, especially in Florida and California.

Belted kingfisher

One of our most conspicuous birds, full of character. Look out for a blue-and-white bird with a shaggy crest and a blue breast-band (male) or chestnut one (female). Often flies along rivers or streams, uttering its rattling call.

Mallard

Our largest dabbling duck, found throughout North America, and especially common in towns and cities. Male is very handsome, with a bottle green head, magenta breast, and white collar; female is speckled brown with purplish patch bordered with white on the wing. Both have yellow bills.

American black duck

Resembles a small, very dark female mallard with a darker brown body (appears blackish at a distance) and a paler brown head. Males and females are identical. Found mainly in the eastern United States, though declining.

American coot

Not a duck, though it looks like one! This member of the rail family is basically grayish black, with a black head, and white bill topped with a small red knob. Common on ponds and marshes throughout the United States.

Ruddy duck

A tiny but colorful little duck: males have chestnut plumage offset by white cheeks and black cap—and amazing bright blue bill! Females are brown with pale stripes along face. Both have distinctive sticking-up tail, which the male uses in courtship displays.

Northern pintail

This elegant, slim duck is one of our most widespread and most striking. Male has a gray body, white breast, and chocolate brown head; female is brown, with long neck and speckled plumage. Male also has a distinctive long tail, which gives the species its name.

Go pishing to attract small birds

Yes, that's right—go pishing. It may sound rude, and you may get some funny looks doing it, but it's the best way I know to get really up-close-and-personal with some of our smallest birds.

You start by visiting a town or city park, or a patch of woods on a day in fall or winter—generally coldest days are best.

Listen for tiny, high-pitched noises—the calls made by birds like chickadees and titmice as they try to keep in contact with one another. At this time of year, they tend to travel in flocks—it's the best way to find food and avoid danger. The more pairs of eyes, the more food they can find, and the more likely they are to spot a predator and sound the alarm.

When you've heard the sounds, follow them until they get loud enough to hear quite clearly. Then stand still, and make a loud "pish-pish-pish" sound, repeating yourself and making sure the "shhhhh" really sounds hissy.

At this point, you may start to feel a bit silly, especially if any-one's watching you. But bear with me—it really does work. If you keep on pishing, eventually the birds will start to get curious and come to investigate.

After a minute or two, you'll notice a movement in the leaves in front of you, and a tiny bird will pop out. If you keep pishing he'll usually stay still for a moment or two, probably wondering why this huge, strange-looking creature (you) is making such a peculiar noise. He may even be joined by a few of his fellows.

As you watch them, think about the lives these little birds lead. Every day they must eat more than one-third of their own body weight—just to survive. So once you've had a good look at them, let them carry on their way—they've got work to do.

The theory behind pishing is that the birds think you're another bird and have found a predator (perhaps an owl or a hawk) and is seeing it off, using a hissing, scolding call. Oddly, instead of flying away, they come to check out the threat for themselves.

Search for hibernating butterflies

Butterflies in winter? Surely that can't be right. Well, yes, it's true that many species of butterfly either head south in the fall to spend the winter in warmer climes, or pass the cold weather as caterpillars or in their chrysalis stage. But several kinds, including some of the anglewings, do spend the winter hibernating as adults.

To do so, they seek out quiet, sheltered places. Look for them in your garage, garden shed, or any other outbuilding. They can be tricky to spot—they rest with their wings closed, so their bright colors don't usually show. Search for them high up, where the wall meets the ceiling, or perhaps in a corner of a room.

If you do find a hibernating butterfly make sure you don't disturb it—if they wake up too early, when the weather is still cold, they will lose valuable energy and may not be able to survive the rest of the winter.

And although you may be tempted to buy a specially made butterfly hibernation box, the butterflies usually ignore them and find a place that suits them—so don't waste your money!

The color in a butterfly's wings is not always what it seems. Some butterflies reflect light in a way that produces new colors—known as iridescence—which can be seen only from a certain angle.

Go beachcombing along the tide line

One of the most satisfying and enjoyable things you can do along our coasts is to go beachcombing: simply taking a walk along the tide line to see what you can find. Of course you can do this at any time of year, but there's something special about being out in the middle of winter, when the summer vacation crowds have long gone, and the beach is deserted.

Almost anything found at sea can eventually wash up on the tide line, and over time, much of it does. There may be natural objects such as seashells, the bodies of dead birds or other sea creatures, or man-made objects such as remains from a shipwreck—or, more likely nowadays, the ever increasing mountain of plastic rubbish that gets dumped at sea.

Although you may occasionally come across something you would rather not see, beachcombing is endlessly unpredictable and fascinating; you really never do know quite what you'll find, even if you walk along the same stretch of tide line every day of your life.

The best time to go beachcombing is on a falling tide, when the seas reveal their secrets. Every tide brings new objects—the "flotsam and jetsam" of the modern world. Flotsam and jetsam are used interchangeably to describe anything washed up on the beach—although strictly speaking flotsam is any object that floats (that is, something washed off a ship or shipwreck), while jetsam is an object that has been deliberately thrown overboard by the crew of a boat or ship.

Below are some natural objects to look for and collect

* Pebbles: everything from rounded ones made smooth by eons of being beaten by the waves to sharp, jagged lumps of rock recently broken off the cliffs by autumn gales.
* Seashells: from common or garden cockles, mussels, periwinkles, and whelks to the more exotic-looking razor shells and scallops.
* Cuttlefish bones: glowing white among the sand or shingle, these are also a common find, as are "mermaid's purses," the egg cases of the ray or dogfish (a relative of the shark).
* Seaweed: great strands of kelp, some many yards long; or bladder wrack, a brownish green seaweed usually found on rocks whose air chambers make a satisfying sound when you squeeze them between your finger and thumb until they pop.

* Driftwood: not strictly natural, as it may well be a piece of decking or other wood from a ship. But the effect of the sea will often create a really beautiful object you can take home and use as the basis for a work of art.
* Semiprecious stones: lumps of amber (fossilized pine resin about forty million years old) or smaller colorful gems.
* Live creatures: stranded jellyfish are common, especially after winter storms.

Tips

* Don't go beachcombing on a rising tide—you may get cut off as the water comes up the beach.
* Wear shoes with treads, water shoes, or Tevas—rocks can be very slippery.
* Turn over rocks to see what's underneath, but make sure you put the rock back in the same place afterward.
* Check out the tide line itself, as well as rock pools.
* Dig down into the sand to see what you can find.
* Take a bucket to fill with seawater so you can observe any living creatures you find.
* Once you've finished looking, put live creatures back where you found them—the next tide will usually wash them back to sea.
* Be careful near the underside of cliffs—rocks frequently fall, especially in winter.

The lower forty-eight U.S. states (excluding Alaska and Hawaii) have a total coastline just over 6,000 miles long—but if you add Alaska and Hawaii, that figure more than doubles, to more than 12,300 miles! Yet this pales in comparison with Canada, which boasts the world's longest coastline: a mind-boggling 126,300 miles—more than ten times that of the United States.

Watch the sun rise and set on the same day

A survey in Japan (the land of the rising sun) found that over half the nation's children had never seen the sun rise or set. Yet this is a great way to get to understand the daily rhythms of the universe—and it has the added advantage that you can do it almost anywhere.

Choose a day in the middle of winter, when you won't have to get up too early or go to bed too late. Check the weather forecast the day before—you'll need high pressure with clear skies, so you can be sure the sun's rays will get through.

Pick a place with a bit of height—a small hill is ideal. Check out the times of sunrise and sunset in a newspaper or on the Internet, and make sure you get up early enough to be situated a few minutes before the sun comes over the horizon. Wrap up warmly, take some food and drink, and wait for the first rays to appear.

In the evening, go back to the same location—but remember that the sun sets in the opposite half of the sky; rising in the east and setting in the west. What you've just witnessed is the turning of Earth, which rotates through a full cycle every twenty-four hours and gives us day and night.

The sun is about 93 million miles away from Earth, but the moon is only about 250,000 miles away. Yet to us, they usually appear roughly the same size. This amazing coincidence is because the sun is roughly 360 times farther away than the moon, and also about 400 times the size.

Go swimming in the sea in winter

Although it may seem bizarre, the seas around our coasts are warmer in December than in April. That's because while the sea warms up more slowly than the land in spring and summer, it also cools down more slowly. So even on Christmas Day the sea temperature may be higher than you think.

Another advantage of swimming in winter is that because the air temperature is cooler, the sea will seem warmer—think about how cold it feels when you plunge into the waves on a hot summer's day and you'll see what I mean.

There is a long tradition of winter swimming in the northeastern United States, started by immigrants from Scandinavia and northern Europe, where swimming in winter has long been known to have health benefits.

These so-called polar bear clubs hold regular events—either just once a year (usually on New Year's Day) or every weekend during the winter months. They often raise money for charity by doing so. If you'd like to take part, check out clubs in your neighborhood, where you can get the best advice on how to take the plunge!

The honored title of the oldest winter swimming club in the United States is a matter of passionate debate. The Coney Island Polar Bears were founded in 1903, while Boston's L Street Brownies did their first official swim on New Year's Day, 1904. However there is evidence that the Boston swimmers were swimming in the harbor in winter as early as 1888, perhaps even 1865.

How to identify . . .
marine mammals

Some of North America's most impressive and fascinating mammals have evolved to live their lives in one of the world's most hostile environments—the sea. These include the true ocean-going mammals—whales, dolphins, and porpoises (known collectively as cetaceans)—as well as others that divide their lives between the sea and the land, such as seals, sea lions, and the charismatic sea otter.

A vacation by the sea—on the Pacific, Atlantic, or Gulf coasts of North America—is a great way to catch sight of these wonderful creatures. Some can be seen easily from the shore, such as seals and sea lions lolling about on rocks. Others only live out in the open ocean, so you'll need to take a trip out to sea to catch up with them.

marine mammals

North Atlantic right whale

One of our rarest and most endangered whales, with only a few hundred remaining because of hunting. More likely to come close to shore than other whales, so may be seen off the Atlantic Coast, especially Maine. Large and stocky, with a big head, smallish flippers, and no back fin.

Gray whale

Medium-size (up to forty-five feet long), dark gray all over, with no back fin and very small flippers. Often seen in large groups off the Pacific Coast, as it undertakes one of the longest migrations on the planet, heading north to breed.

Humpback whale

Medium-size (up to fifty feet long), with obvious contrast between dark grayish black back and white undersides. Very long flippers and the distinctive hump from which it gets its name. Often seen leaping out of the water and hitting the surface of the sea with its tail. Can be seen off all coasts, though more regular in the Pacific.

Orca

This fearsome predator—weighing up to six tons—is also one of the fastest sea creatures, easily able to chase down its prey of seals, seabirds, or fish, or even occasionally large whales. Regularly seen offshore from Pacific and Atlantic coasts.

Northern elephant seal

The largest seal in North America, with males weighing in at a colossal five thousand pounds (more than three times the average weight of the female) and up to fifteen feet long. Easily told apart from other seals and sea lions by its huge size and the male's distinctively shaped nose. Found off California.

Common bottle-nosed dolphin

The classic dolphin, familiar from captivity, can also be seen in its true wild state along both our coasts. Pale gray in color, with a distinctive short "nose" and large head. Often rides in the bow wave of boats.

Harbor porpoise

One of the smallest marine mammals, with a distinctive rounded head and nose, and dark above and pale below. Often seen in harbors, sometimes even in river estuaries.

California sea lion

Unlike seals, sea lions have large, flexible front flippers, enabling them to walk on land more easily. Although clumsy on land they are graceful in the water. Found all along the Pacific Coast.

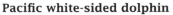

Pacific white-sided dolphin

Along with its relative, the Atlantic white-sided dolphin, it is a common, sociable animal, often seen in large pods. Found along the whole Pacific Coast. Identified by its contrasting pattern of dark above, white below, and pale gray sides.

Manatee

This rare and unusual mammal, also known as a sea cow, lives up to this name by grazing on aquatic vegetation in shallow waters, off the Gulf and Atlantic coasts of the United States. Now very rare and found mainly in Florida.

Harbor seal

The commonest seal, and the most terrestrial, spending much of its life basking on rocks or beaches before swimming off on a rising tide to hunt for fish. Yet in the sea it is transformed into a ruthless predator, able to dive to depths of over three hundred feet.

Sea otter

This delightful creature is, unlike its riverine cousin, almost always found in the water, only coming ashore in very bad weather. Our smallest marine mammal, it feeds by diving for shellfish such as abalone and then cracking them open by hitting them against a rock on their belly! Found all along the Pacific Coast of North America.

Look for winter wildlife

Although we think of spring and summer as the best times to scout for wildlife, there's plenty of activity in winter as well—you just need to know where to look. And there are some creatures that may be easier to see in this season than at any other time of year—especially after snow, when you may be able to find and identify animals by following their tracks.

* Elk: this large deer forages for food in mountain meadows during the summer, but as winter approaches they usually move down to lower altitudes, such as valleys and the wooded slopes of foothills, where they are often easier to see. Mainly found in the western United States, especially along the Rockies.
* Snowshoe hare: this northern species has the incredible ability to change color from summer to winter, molting its blackish brown fur into a pure white coat (apart from the black tips of its ears). Its forest habitat means it is hard to see at any time of the year, but harsh winter weather may make it more visible as it forages for food. Mainly confined to northern states.
* Snowy owl: this bird of the High Arctic turns nomadic in fall and winter and, depending on fluctuations in its food supply, may wander farther south at this time of year. Often hunts by day.
* Snow goose: this classic bird of the North migrates long distances during the fall to spend the winter in southern havens, where there is plenty of food. Look for them as they travel south in the fall, and check out vast flocks on their prairie wintering grounds.

Take part in the Christmas Bird Count

For many of us, Christmas is a time for getting together with our families, exchanging gifts, and enjoying good food and festive cheer. But for the birds it is one of the toughest times of year, as they struggle to survive the cold and get enough food during the short winter days to survive.

Although the days are short in winter, especially in the northern United States, they provide us with a golden opportunity to get out in the field and enjoy close-up views of birds. So why not take part in the oldest and biggest bird survey anywhere in the world—the annual Christmas Bird Count?

You'll not only have a great time and see some wonderful birds, but you'll also be contributing to the longest continuous set of data on birds in existence, which is used to help understand and conserve our birdlife.

The CBC, as it is usually known, has its origins in the hunting tradition: during the nineteenth century many hunters competed to see how many birds they could kill in a single day.

Pioneering birder and conservationist Frank Chapman wanted to channel all this effort into conserving America's birds rather than killing them. He understood that mobilizing North America's amateur birders would be a great way to learn more about the status and distribution of our avian wildlife.

The very first CBC took place on Christmas Day, 1900, and involved just 27 observers in 25 different locations, mostly in the northeastern United States. By 1909 more than 200 people were taking part, logging over 150,000 individual birds; and in 1939, 2,000 counters logged over two million birds.

Counts now take place in 17 different countries as far away as Colombia. In 2008, the 109th annual Christmas Bird Count, well over 50,000 people in more than 2,100 locations recorded an extraordinary total of 65,480,848 individual birds.

The record single count in the United States was logged in Matagorda County, Texas, on December 19, 2005—an incredible total of 250 different species!

The rules are simple

* Each count must take place in a circle with a diameter of fifteen miles.
* At least ten volunteers must be involved.
* The counters may split up and follow different routes to maximize coverage within each circle.
* They must count every individual bird they see—not just each species.
* The count can be held on any day between December 14 and January 5.
* Anyone can take part, so long as they pay an entry fee of $5. If you are under nineteen years old you get to participate for free! Check out the CBC Web site http://www.audubon.org/bird/cbc/getinvolved.html for more information.

Make maple syrup candy

This mouthwatering recipe was passed on to me by the author Sue Halpern. Sue and her husband, the environmental writer Bill McKibben, live in Vermont, where collecting maple syrup is one of the traditional outdoor activities of late winter and early spring. But if you don't live in a place where you can collect the syrup yourself, just use the stuff you get at your local store—but make sure you choose good-quality syrup for the very best flavor.

One Christmas Sue and her daughter Sophie made this delicious maple syrup candy for their family and friends. As Sue remarks, when you make this candy, it's time to alert all dentists!

What you need

- Grade A maple syrup, if available
- A heavy-bottomed quart-size pot
- A small pat of butter
- A candy thermometer
- A metal bread pan or other pan with high sides
- A large spoon
- Pliable rubber or plastic molds

This is one of those recipes that looks quite easy but requires a bit of finesse, practice, and good luck. Make sure your molds are clean and dry, and that you have adult supervision.

1. Pour syrup into the pot so it's about one-third full.
2. Add the pat of butter.
3. Attach the candy thermometer to the side of the pot so you can keep track of the syrup temperature.
4. Turn on the heat up to high.
5. When the syrup reaches 240°F, remove it from the heat. (It will be boiling a lot.)
6. Pour it into the pan with high sides, and when it cools to 110°F begin to stir it vigorously with the big spoon until it changes color, lightening and becoming opaque, and until its consistency becomes somewhat plastic.
7. Now pour it quickly into the molds, smoothing out the top. (This is done best as a two-person operation, with one person pouring and the other one smoothing.)
8. Wait 10 to 15 minutes, and then pop the candies out of the mold.
9. Let them cool. Eat and enjoy!

Maple syrup is probably the oldest commodity in North America, having been harvested by Native Americans in the Great Lakes region and New England for centuries. The high sugar content of the syrup (more than 66 percent) meant that it was a very valuable source of energy, especially during a hard winter.

Six things to do when it snows

Despite global climate change, it does still snow in the United States. Indeed, if you live in the eastern states, as far south as Washington, D.C., it's a rare winter that passes without at least one heavy snowfall. And even if you live in the snow-free South, you should always be prepared for the unexpected appearance of white stuff falling from the sky.

Make a snowman

* Start by rolling the snow into a large snowball—at least three feet across, if you can manage it. Keep patting the snow as you roll it, to pack it in as densely as possible. This will be the main "body" of your snowman.
* Then roll some more snow into a slightly smaller ball—about eighteen inches across—this will form the upper body.
* Finally make a third, even smaller, ball—this time about eight to twelve inches across—for the snowman's head.
* Put the medium-size ball on top of the large one, pushing down firmly to stick the two together (but not so hard that the whole thing collapses). Then place the smallest ball firmly on top of the other two.
* Take two pieces of dark stone, pebbles, or coins (in my day we used coal, but you might find that a bit hard to get hold of) and push them into the head to make the eyes.
* Push a carrot into the head below the "eyes" to make the nose.
* Put more small stones or pebbles in a semicircle beneath the carrot to make the snowman's mouth.
* Give him a hat and wrap a scarf around his neck to keep him nice and warm.

And if you're enjoying an unexpected snowfall someplace where you don't usually see it, do it all as quickly as you can before the snow starts to melt!

Catch a snowflake on your tongue

There can be few experiences more pure and simple than opening your mouth when it's snowing and allowing the snowflakes to fall upon your tongue.

Look at a snowflake through a magnifying glass

It's often said that no two snowflakes are alike, and while this is technically correct at the microscopic level, to the naked eye many snowflakes do look remarkably similar. But if you look really closely at snowflakes through a magnifying glass you will begin to see the complex, beautiful patterns of these six-sided crystals of ice.

Make snow angels

This is fun to do—provided you're dressed warmly, ideally in waterproof clothing so you don't get soaked.

* Find a nice, even patch of pure, white snow, which people and dogs haven't discovered yet.
* Lie flat on your back, as carefully as you can, trying not to disturb the snow around your body.

* Slowly stretch out your arms and legs—then move your arms
  up and down across the snow in an arc from your waist to
  almost (but not quite) above your head, and move your legs in
  and out from straight down to stretched out as far as you can.
* Get up, again as carefully as possible, and step back. There, on
  the snow, is your very own "snow angel."

Slide down a slope on a tray or garbage bag

Sledding and tobogganing are great activities—all you need is a hill. If you haven't got a proper sled, what can you do? Well, you could try:

* A large wooden or plastic tray.
* A plastic garbage bag—the thick ones are the best; the thin ones are likely to rip.
* A large cardboard box—folded flat and taped up with any strong sticky tape.

And, of course . . .

Have a snowball fight

* Roll up some snow, pressing it as hard as you can as you pack it together into a ball.
* Throw it at your friend/brother/sister/mom/dad/grandson/ daughter/boss/the mailman.*
* Run or duck!

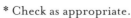

* Check as appropriate.

How to identify . . .
large mammals

North America is home to some of the most majestic and impressive large mammals on the planet, ranging from the common and familiar coyote and bobcat to the rare and elusive lynx and grizzly bear.

Seeing these creatures is always a privilege and sometimes quite difficult. Those animals that hunt for a living try to keep hidden and are often most active at dawn and dusk, and in wild, remote places. Their prey species, meanwhile, can also be elusive, as they tend to regard human beings with suspicion: after all, these are also the animals the Wild West pioneers hunted, sometimes, in the case of the American bison, almost to extinction.

But with a combination of effort, guidance, and a little luck many of these animals will allow themselves to be seen, and you will have a truly awe-inspiring experience that you will remember for the rest of your life.

How to identify . . .
large mammals

Coyote

Much smaller than a wolf and resembling a large domestic dog, coyotes are one of our most adaptable and widespread large mammals. They are able to hunt and scavenge for food in a wide range of habitats, including towns and cities. Still heavily persecuted, yet a true survivor, with a fascinating family life.

Grizzly bear

North America's largest mammal, a full-grown male grizzly can tip the scales at over two thousand pounds, and stand nine feet tall. Also known in the coastal parts of its range as the brown bear, the grizzly was once widespread across the continent, but hunting forced it back into its northwestern stronghold. Swims well, often wading into water to catch salmon.

Gray wolf

One of North America's best-known animals, with a host of stories, myths, and folktales surrounding it. Gray wolves are sociable animals, hunting in a pack, and with a clear pecking order among the pack members. Mainly found in the northern part of the continent.

Moose

North America's—and indeed the world's—largest deer, with males standing over seven feet tall and weighing up to 1,300 pounds. Also sports the most impressive set of antlers. Mainly nocturnal, though can also be seen by day; mostly in the northern part of the continent.

American bison

Once roaming the plains of the Wild West in herds numbering millions of animals, by 1900 the bison had been hunted virtually to extinction. Nowadays numbers have recovered a little, but they can only be found in a handful of refuges, mainly in the North and West.

Elk

A large and majestic-looking deer, whose males sport a fine set of antlers, which they use to fight one another for females during the annual rut. Usually found in large herds in open habitats, they are also found in hilly areas of the North and West.

Mountain lion

Also known as the cougar or puma, this is a solitary hunter, rarely seen, as it often stalks its prey by night. The commonest cat in the New World, its large size, pale brown fur, and small head are very distinctive. Mainly found in the western states.

Wolverine

This bearlike carnivore (though considerably smaller and with a bushier tail) is in fact related to weasels and otters. It roams the far north in search of animal prey, sometimes forcing larger predators, such as bears, from a kill. Dark brown, with distinctive yellowish buff stripes along sides of back.

White-tailed deer

By far the most common and widespread North American deer, found in forested and scrubby areas throughout the continent. Males have branching antlers and are larger than females. Varying in color and size, they tend to be brownish red in summer and brownish gray in winter.

Bobcat

Medium-size cat with a distinctive short tail and short, tufted ears. Similar to the lynx but with shorter ears, a longer tail, and distinctive white with black spotting on its underparts. Found throughout much of the United States, and more likely to be seen than other cats.

Black bear

Smaller and darker than the grizzly bear, up to six feet tall and weighing up to nine hundred pounds. Sometimes shows white chest patch. Often active by day, foraging for food or climbing trees. More widespread than the grizzly bear, it can be found in mountainous areas throughout North America.

Pronghorn

Its scientific name means "antelope-goat," though in fact the pronghorn is neither and has its own unique family. Found in open grassy areas and deserts, and confined to western states, where it is much less common than it once was.

Lynx

Has distinctive, long tufted ears, a short black-tipped tail, and a thicker winter coat than the bobcat, which it resembles. Confined to the North, having declined in numbers and range due to hunting.

Winter weather lore

Watching the behavior of wildlife in winter is a really good way to predict the weather—at least for the next day or two. Birds, in particular, will move south and west in large numbers to avoid a sudden spell of very cold weather, since snow and ice make it difficult for them to find food.

So watch out for large flocks of birds flying overhead—particularly geese and ducks, which will often move ahead of falling snow. But as long as the water they feed on remains ice free, they will sometimes stay put, if they're still able to feed.

There is a whole range of sayings and beliefs that are said to predict the long-term weather for the coming winter. These include:

* Listening for when the katydids begin to sing. The first frost is supposed to occur exactly ninety days later.
* Count the number of days from the first snowfall until Christmas. This is supposedly the same number of snowfalls you will see during the rest of the winter.
* If your dog howls at a full moon, this is supposed to mean early snowfalls that winter.

And looking ahead to the coming spring:

* A white Christmas is said to foretell a green (that is, fine and warm) Easter.

Unfortunately, as with all long-term weather forecasting based on folklore, the chances of any of these forecasts being accurate are roughly fifty-fifty—which means you might as well toss a coin to decide what to believe!

Meanwhile, during harsh winter weather, it's vital to give birds and other backyard wildlife a helping hand . . .

* Keep your bird feeders full with high-energy foods such as sunflower hearts, mixed seeds, and fat balls.
* If it snows really heavily, put out food on bird tables and on a tray on the ground for birds that don't come to hanging feeders.
* Make sure your birdbath is kept full with water. If it's iced over, pour cold (not hot) water into it until the ice melts.
* If you have a pond in your backyard, make a hole in the ice so that birds and other animals can drink from it.

And finally, as you wait for the snowdrops to bloom, the butterflies to appear, and the swallows to return, remember a hopeful line from the poet Shelley: "If Winter comes, can Spring be far behind?"

Useful contacts

American Birding Association
4945 North 30th Street, Suite 200
Colorado Springs, CO 80919
Tel: (800) 850-2473 or (719) 578-9703
www.aba.org

American Museum of Natural History
Central Park West at 79th Street
New York, NY 10024
Tel: (212) 769-5100
www.amnh.org

National Audubon Society
225 Varick Street, 7th Floor
New York, NY 10014
Tel: (212) 979-3000
www.audubon.org

National Geographic Society
1145 17th Street N.W.
Washington, D.C. 20036
Tel: (800) 647-5463
www.nationalgeographic.com

U.S. Fish and Wildlife Service
Tel: (800) 344-9453
www.fws.gov

Wilderness Society
1615 M Street N.W.
Washington, D.C. 20036
Tel: (800) 843-9453
www.wilderness.org

Wildlife Conservation Society
2300 Southern Boulevard
Bronx, NY 10460
Tel: (718) 220-5100
www.wcs.org

World Wildlife Fund
1250 24th Street N.W.
P.O. Box 97180
Washington, D.C. 20090-7180
Tel: (202) 293-4800
www.worldwildlife.org

Further reading

Here is a selection of the best field guides, books, and magazines that will help you make the most of wildlife watching in the United States—at any time of year! Most titles will be obtainable in bookstores or by mail order from Internet suppliers.

General

North American Wildlife (Reader's Digest)

Backyard wildlife

Peterson Field Guides: Feeder Birds of Eastern North America, by Roger Tory Peterson (Houghton Mifflin)

Birds

National Wildlife Federation Field Guide to Birds of North America, by Edward S. Brinkley (Sterling)

National Geographic Field Guide to the Birds of North America, by Jon L. Dunn and Jonathan Alderfer (National Geographic Society)

Kaufman Field Guide to Birds of North America, by Kenn Kaufman (Turtleback)

The Sibley Guide to Birds, by David Sibley (Sibley Guides)

The Sibley Guide to Bird Life and Behavior, by David Sibley (Sibley Guides)

Mammals

Kaufman Focus Guides: Mammals of North America, by Nora Bowers, Rick Bowers, and Kenn Kaufman (Houghton Mifflin)

Princeton Field Guides: Mammals of North America, by Roland W. Kays and Don E. Wilson (Princeton University Press)

National Geographic Book of Mammals, National Geographic Society (National Geographic Children's Books)

Peterson Field Guides: Mammals of North America, by Fiona A. Reid (Houghton Mifflin)

Tracking and the Art of Seeing: How to Read Animal Tracks and Sign, by Paul Rezendes (Collins Reference)

National Audubon Society Field Guide to North American Mammals, by John O. Whitaker (Knopf)

The Smithsonian Book of North American Mammals, by Don E. Wilson and Sue Ruff (University of British Columbia Press)

Reptiles and amphibians

Peterson Field Guides: Reptiles and Amphibians: Eastern/Central North America, by Roger Conant and Joseph T. Collins (Houghton Mifflin)

National Audubon Society Field Guide to Reptiles and Amphibians: North America (Knopf)

A Golden Guide: Reptiles of North America, by Hobart Smith (Golden Books)

Insects

Peterson Field Guides: Insects, by Donald J. Borror and Richard E. White (Houghton Mifflin)

Kaufman Field Guide to Insects of North America, by Eric R. Eaton and Kenn Kaufman (Turtleback)

Plants

The Jepson Manual: Higher Plants of California, by James C. Hickman
(University of California Press)
Peterson Field Guides: Wildflowers, by Roger Tory Peterson and
Margaret McKenny (Houghton Mifflin)
Peterson Field Guides: Edible Wild Plants: Eastern/Central North America, by
Lee Allen Peterson (Houghton Mifflin)
Peterson Field Guides: Trees and Shrubs, by George A. Petrides
(Houghton Mifflin)
National Audubon Society Field Guide to North American Wildflowers (Knopf)

Acknowledgments

During a lifetime's watching and enjoying wildlife, many people have helped me learn about the natural world—to all of whom, too many to thank individually, I send my grateful thanks.

At Harmony Books, my editor, John Glusman, has provided just the right measure of encouragement and objectivity, and the book has benefited hugely from his editorial skill, vision, and patience. I should also like to thank Kate Kennedy, Anne Berry, Domenica Alioto, Maria Elias, Luisa Francavilla, Christine Tanigawa, Kira Walton, Campbell Wharton, and Shaye Areheart.

Special thanks to the natural history consultant, Neil Duncan of the American Museum of Natural History in New York City, and to the artists Patricia J. Wynne (color plates) and Nicole Heidaripour (line drawings), whose art both graces and elevates the text.

My agents, Broo Doherty and Jonathan Lyons, deserve very special thanks for their support and encouragement throughout this project.

I hope that my children, David, James, Charlie, George, and Daisy, will continue to grow to love being out and about and enjoying nature for the rest of their lives.

And finally, to my darling wife, Suzanne, who has opened my eyes to what really matters in life, and who will always be there with me, watching and enjoying the wild world.